BUYING AND SELLING A HOME

with

TOM TYNAN

A HOMEOWNERS GUIDE TO SURVIVAL

SWAN PUBLISHING

TEXAS • CALIFORNIA • NEW YORK

Author: Tom Tynan
Editors: George Tynan and Pete Billac
Layout design: Sharon Davis
Architectural consultant: Paul Titterington
Cover photo: Jennifer Lamb
Cover design: Mark Fornataro

Books by Tom Tynan:

VOL 1 HOME IMPROVEMENT, *Homeowners Most Often Asked Questions*

VOL 2 BUILDING AND REMODELING, *A Homeowners Guide to Getting Started*

VOL 3 BUYING AND SELLING A HOME, *A Homeowners Guide to Survival*

VOL 4 STEP BY STEP, *A Homeowners Guide to Solving Bigger Problems* (Due in January 1996)

Copyright @ December 1995
Tom Tynan and Swan Publishing
Library of Congress Catalog Number 94-69064
ISBN 0-943629-13-6

BUYING AND SELLING A HOME is available in quantity discounts through: SWAN PUBLISHING COMPANY, 126 Live Oak, Suite 100, Alvin, TX 77511. (713) 388-2547 or FAX (713) 585-3738.

Printed in the United States of America

Here I am again, trying to "get the word" out to my radio listeners, television watchers and friends who call into my program—actually, to everyone who is buying a home or selling a home.

This is my third book in one single year, and probably my favorite because it seems that everyone during their lifetime either buys a home or sells a home. I've done both—several times—and I've also built a lot of homes and have been in this "home business" of buying, selling, remodeling or constructing for just about all of my adult life.

This book, I vow to you, will save you more money and aggravation if you are buying a home or selling a home than any book I've ever read. I'm not talking from vanity, it's fact. I get down to the basics of what to look for when buying, what to do when selling, and I take you up through methods of financing. If you read it and follow what I've learned and gleaned from experts, you will save time, stress and money. I can't promise you more than that.

Tom Tynan

DEDICATION

To my grandfather, James G. Mascelli, and to my grandmother, Theresa Ann Mascelli. You never turned your back on me, even during my lowest point in life. Whatever I have and am, I owe to you.

When I close my eyes to sleep, I see both of you smiling and comforting me. You were loving, caring, supportive and always instilling confidence in me. I wish you were alive to see me during these successful and happy times. God, how I love you and I miss you both.

ACKNOWLEDGEMENTS

Thanks to SUZANNE DEBIEN, agent of Henry S. Miller Realtors for her patience with my editor and her input.

Also to PAULA GINSBURG, senior loan officer for First Financial Mortgage for her time and willingness to share pertinent information that made this book possible.

And, thanks to my editor and friend, PETE BILLAC, who thought what I had to say was what you, my readers, would like to learn about.

To JIMMY, AMANDA and JOHN, for their participation in the cover photo. It only took mommy 3 roles of film to get one good shot. Daddy is a builder but couldn't nail you in place. Finally, the three of you paused for a moment, **at the same time!**

INTRODUCTION

This book is directed toward those who are buying or selling a home and is split into three parts; Part I talks of **BUYING A HOME**; Part II, **SELLING A HOME**; and Part III is information for **BUYERS AND SELLERS**. You can bet that Tom holds nothing back in telling you facts that many others sidestep. If he likes (or doesn't like) something, he'll tell you exactly the way it is. He is unafraid to voice his opinions openly.

If you already have Volume 1 of his books **HOME IMPROVEMENT—Homeowner's Most Often Asked Questions**, you'll have answers to most of the troublesome things you'll need to know if you already own a home; how to repair and maintain it doing much of the work yourself. This book has sold over 100,000 copies in 14 months and is about to go into its fifth printing.

Should you have his second book, Volume 2, **BUILDING AND REMODELING—A Homeowner's Guide To Getting Started,** you'll be able to decide **if**, **why** and **how** to build and/or remodel on your own. Tom tells you the easiest and best way to do these things.

In this book, Volume 3, **BUYING AND SELLING A HOME**, Tom gives you the methods of choosing a home and how to take it from start to finish. He talks about what to look for, who to get help from, which papers are necessary to fill out, how to obtain a mortgage and which kind to choose. He tells everything a new homeowner (even a second and third-time homeowner) needs to know.

If you're selling a home, Tom gives you a complete rundown on the repairs to make (and those you shouldn't make) in order to ready this home for a buyer. He tells how to "set the stage" to make your home more appealing and some little secrets he's gleaned from realtors, homeowners and from his own experiences.

Yes, welcome to the world of Tom Tynan. His life's goal seem to be to help others in any and every facet of dealing with a home whether it's buying, selling, financing, mortgaging, repairing, maintaining, remodeling or building. You'll learn from, save money on, and enjoy reading this book. I guarantee it!

Pete Billac
Editor and Publisher

TABLE OF CONTENTS

Part I
BUYING A HOME

Chapter 1   You've decided to buy   13
Chapter 2   Working with a realtor   26
Chapter 3   How to secure financing   40
Chapter 4   How to really look for a home   55
Chapter 5   Negotiating the deal   68
Chapter 6   Getting a good inspection   74

Part II
SELLING A HOME

Chapter 7   What is your home worth   85
Chapter 8   Sell by owner or agency   92
Chapter 9   How to prepare your home to sell   99
Chapter 10 Increase the value of your home 115

Part III
BUYERS AND SELLERS

Chapter 11 You've both got to move 121
Chapter 12 Exemptions & taxes after age 65 129

PROLOGUE

Before we get into the various aspects of buying a home, I want each of you contemplating this act to ask yourself one question . . .

SHOULD YOU OWN A HOME

How I want this to read is should **you** own a home? There are instances where people have no need of a home and this isn't only unmarried people without children. Some people simply don't **have** the time or want to **take** the time to own a home because it is a degree of work, unforeseen expense, and some time away from the fun things you enjoy doing. Too, many singles spend their money partying and don't have any savings or credit; to own a home you need some of both.

That's why owning your own home either has to be fun or you have a kid or two and have been evicted from every other place you've lived, and you have no choice; buy a home of your own or sleep under a bridge.

Personally, I like owning a home because I can do with it as I choose. You know, tailor-make it to fit my own comforts. I like the tax write-off, the equity build-up and I like the feeling of permanency. I'm reasonably friendly and I like neighbors who aren't moving every few months or years and I was starting a family so I needed a house.

For those of you who are professional singles well,

I can't generalize or categorize anyone because I know single people who own their own home and I know married couples who live in apartments. It's a decision you have to make for yourself. If you enjoy life not owning, why change? But, if you do decide to let go and buy, let me give you some examples of what not to do from homeowners I know, and knew of.

Before we get down to business, I'd like for those of you who haven't heard any of my radio shows or read any of my books to know a little about my personality. My wife doesn't think I'm funny, funny-looking maybe, but not funny. My editor thinks I have corn-ball jokes and doesn't like the fact that I don't laugh at his.

Throughout this book I try to intersperse it with my own weird sense of humor and I'm just hoping that those of you who buy this book have heard me on the radio or seen me on television and know that I am a bit corn-ball at times. I, personally, get a kick out of my jokes. I laugh at them and I hope you do too.

I have some lines of extra space to make the print come out close to the end on this page and I'll share one of my editor's jokes with you, one he wanted me to say over the air. I refused. I think it's antiquated, not funny and kind of stupid.

"Tom, tell your listeners that to fix their heat exchanger they will need a Henway."
I looked at him and asked, *"What the heck is a Henway?"*
"Maybe 3 or 4 pounds. A rooster usually weighs more."

He laughed for 30 minutes while I just looked at him, dumbfounded. I didn't think it was a bit funny. Does that mean I have a bad sense of humor? Did you laugh?

With this touch of jocularity behind us, it's time to begin the book. I hope you enjoy my humor—wherever it appears—and if you laugh, I'll try to accomplish this without anymore Henway-type jokes. I think all writing should have a degree of humor. I hope you agree with me.

This book is meant to serve as a **guide,** as well as a reminder, of many things you already know. Use it as a checklist, not as a bible. Whether you are buying or selling a home, keep this book close by to look through. There will be things that you forget so open it to the page that deals with your particular problem(s) and start circling or scratching out what you've already done.

I'm also in a bit of trouble with my proof readers and editor as far as putting some words in **BOLD** print! I went overboard with **bold** in my first book and left most of them out in my second. This third book, I feel, is a happy medium with the **bold** letters. It's just that I want to call **immediate** and **unquestionable** attention to several key points and, **I like bold letters on some important words!**

Part I

Chapter 1

YOU'VE DECIDED TO BUY

Let's begin with all the people who are **BUYING A HOME.** I'm going to take you through the entire process, one step at a time, to enable you to get a good home at a good price. Too often, people see the outside glitter and buy on impulse. I'd like you to deal with this academically as well.

Be smart about it. Get out a pad and pencil and begin marking down things. Make a checklist of everything I'm telling you and when you begin house-shopping, bring this book along with you. I want you to look beyond the cheery kitchen, a clean bathroom, book shelves and an old stone fireplace. I want you to buy a home that will last!

Buying your first home can be a delightful experience or it can be total drudgery, all depending upon you. My wife tells me I was absolutely miserable to house-shop with, mainly because I wanted to see everything that was **behind** the walls and inside the "guts" of the house whereas she looked for the practical things like how many bedrooms, the neighborhood, large closets in the master bedroom, a large kitchen, fenced backyard.

I had time to look. We moved in from Florida and lived in the city two years before I began looking for a home. We lived in a comfortable apartment but my wife was now 8 months pregnant with the tallest kid on the front cover. We **had** to find a home.

I house-hunted as much as I could, looking at maybe 10 homes a day. I was looking for a rarity; I wanted the best house I could find in a neighborhood we decided upon at a very inexpensive price. (Doesn't everybody?) I wanted to get everything I could wrapped into one neat package; inexpensive home, good neighborhood, owned by a builder of quality homes with an engineering degree who liked to keep things in perfect working order.

I wanted his wife to be a neat-freak (clean house) and landscape architect (great garden) who loved clothes and never threw away any of them away (large closets) and enjoyed cooking (lots of kitchen space). I hoped they were just offered a million-dollar-a year job in some other country and had to move in three days.

My wife was weary with apartment living and I had just been offered my present radio show with KTRH. Things were looking good. She was ready to settle for just any house that didn't have a leaky roof. I looked at maybe 260 houses. My wife was carrying around that extra 30 or so pounds so I did most of the fast looking. Still, we agreed that we'd look at this academically, **exactly** the way I recommend you do it in Chapter 4, titled, HOW TO **REALLY** LOOK FOR A HOME.

First, I'd like to issue a warning to those of you who shop from the "frill" perspective without being academic. These are but a few actual stories from people who bought a home without checking it out as I advise. They suffered "buyers remorse" quickly. These stories opened my eyes in a big way. I'm using them because it makes a person pay more attention. Perhaps you or someone you know can identify with one of these tales.

Joe and Rita

Joe was transferred to a different state and was anxious to find a house so he could move from the motel and get his family down with him. He went directly to a real estate office to get information; a wise move. Being new in town he knew nothing and sought the advice of those who did and who better than a real estate agent who lived in the city most of their life and could direct him to the price home he could afford in a nice neighborhood?

After spending a few hours in the Realtor's office, Joe took a list of houses he felt were worthwhile looking at and went to see what the houses looked like from the **outside.** So far, so good.

Joe liked the second house he saw. It had been vacant for about two months and the Realtor gave him a key. The electricity was still on and Joe did a fast walk-thru. He turned the lights on and off and they worked. He pulled out the kitchen drawers and they slid in and out easily.

He looked in bedroom closets, turned the air conditioner and heater *on* and *off*, looked at the roof which was about a year old and rushed back to the office to inform the happy agent that he wanted the house.

It was listed for $84,900 and Joe made an offer of $75,000. He was going to surprise Rita and the kids. He knew his wife's likes and the big backyard was perfect for Joey and David; his two boys who were 6 and 9.

The agent drew up the earnest money contract and got a deposit of $500 and said she would get back to him. Joe was thrilled when his offer was accepted and he called Rita. They moved into the house in about three weeks.

To "cut to the meat" of the story, within three months the roof leaked, the heat exchanger cracked, the air-conditioning compressor went out, and bricks fell from inside of the large stone fireplace. The end result was an outlay of cash of $20,000...$19,400 of which the couple didn't have.

Solution

Joe, understandably so, was in a rush. What he **should** have done was to take more time to look closer and not be so anxious. But, Joe is human and hadn't read my book. He should also have hired an inspector. For as little as $250, the inspector could have uncovered these defects. Don't **you** make this mistake!

Russell and Diane

Russell was manager of a restaurant in the city and he and Diane needed to "get away" on weekends to relax in the country. One weekend, while visiting friends at their country place, they spotted a *For Sale* sign on a cute little cabin that looked cozy and cheap. It was a bit run down but nothing that Russ couldn't tinker with and repair while they enjoyed the woods and water away from city life.

It was for sale by the owner and Russ liked that; no real estate commission. So, he telephoned the number on the sign and met with the owner, a likeable guy who was going through a divorce and needed the money. Russ could really get a deal. The asking price was $55,000.

Russ made an offer of $40,000 cash. The man hastily accepted. They drew up the papers and Russ wrote out his check. He knew Diane would be ecstatic. Russ likes deals and he especially liked saving money. Who doesn't?

Russ' banker asked if he had a Title Policy but Russ, feeling a title **search** was sufficient (and far cheaper) went with that. Again, a problem. Get a Title **Policy!** With it, if anything goes wrong, you have legal action against the company issuing the policy!

To shorten a long story, Russ ended up paying $95,000 for the "deal" cabin; the $40,000 he paid to the "nice guy" plus the **original** $55,000 asking price to the recently divorced wife, the one who **owned** the property that a title **search** didn't detect.

Of course, Russ has legal action against the man but where was he? It's been four years and they still haven't found him.

Solution

Take it one step at a time. Do it legally and add in the expense of having a Title **Policy** even if you buy real estate from your relative or best friend. In fact, **especially** if you buy it from a relative. There are "deals" to be had but there is a certain procedure that must be followed or the deal backfires.

Pam and Paul

Pam is Marketing Director for a large radio station and Paul, her husband, works in the hotel business. They have no kids, one dog, some tropical fish and are presently living in a luxury apartment. But, they want to **own** their own high-rise apartment.

It just so happened it was at a time when there were *conversions* going on, you know, when investors were buying apartments or high-rises and converting them over to condominiums. A large company bought Pam and Paul's building and started selling the units as condos.

They offered these units to the tenants first and Pam and Paul were thrilled to now be able to own. They loved their unit and the location, and this was just perfect timing for them.

Happily, they consulted their attorney and papers were drawn. The price was lower than it would ever be, the down payment was reasonable, and their monthly outlay of cash to own rather than rent was cut about 30%. Wow! They were lucky!

They needn't worry about repairs because in the condominium contract, the roof, driveway, underground garage, elevators and everything outside the walls of their unit would be shared by the 175 owners. The halls and lobby were air conditioned but this too would be paid from the small extra maintenance payment, again, equally shared by 174 other people.

This was true but . . . in their haste they neglected to deal **academically** with it. They never realized that the new owners of the entire building, charlatans all, gave the average "common area" (area shared by all) air conditioning bills during a six month span that included the **winter** months!

Nor did the sellers point out that the AC units themselves have leaks. The compressors had to be replaced and the heating unit was about to wave bye-bye to the *world-of-the-working* and that the unit to their right was sold to four members of a rock band.

Within six months the "shared expenses" of repairing the items (including one elevator cable and motor) came out to be $417,000. Let's see, split 175 ways came out to be a bit over $3,500 for Pam and Paul.

For you accountants and math teachers, I know 175 divided into $417,00 is $2,382 but, Pam and Paul owned a **two bedroom** unit and the amount is equated by square footage. Since 100 of the units were one-bedroom wit less square footage, Pam and Paul with their larger unit had to "bite the bullet" and pay more.

Solution

If you're not using a licensed real estate agent, if you don't pay for an inspector who deals with these things, or if you haven't hired a **real estate attorney** to draw up papers, at least read this book over and over, turning to the chapters that deal **specifically** with what you plan to buy.

I might have said this in one of my other books but it is important enough to repeat. "There are only two kinds of people who get ripped off; the greedy and/or the uninformed." Be willing to pay for what you get and be **informed!** Take time in making decisions that involve a lot of money.

The advice in this book isn't only for those who want to buy a residence in a neighborhood, but also condominium apartments, town homes, beach cottages, hunting cabins and time-share units. Most of the rules I list are the same with few exceptions.

Ben and Lois

Ben is 27 and Lois is 25. They each work. Ben is a policeman and Lois is a secretary in a law firm. They've been married two years and Lois is expecting. I guess I should say "expecting a baby" and not just "expecting"; she could be expecting a new car for her birthday but that is not going to happen, at least not this year because they are planning to buy a home.

Lois wants to live near her family in the city and Ben wants a home in the country. They had to compromise so they moved to the suburbs, not far from Lois' parents and with not as much land as Ben would have liked.

They decided to rent the home on a lease/purchase option that gave them 2 years to make up their minds to either buy or vacate. The problem was, they waited **too long** to make their decision. There was but one month left on the lease for them to exercise their option and the owners had them over the proverbial barrel.

The owners wife wanted to sell "as is" but the mortgage company would not allow them to sell in that condition; the mortgage company wanted the necessary repairs made **prior** to making a loan.

You had never seen so much scuffling; inspectors and inspections, repairs and remodeling, changes, decisions, arguments and disagreements between buyers and sellers, sellers and sellers, buyers and buyers and buyers and neighbors. I was the neighbor.

I knew the sellers because I had lived next to them for over 4 years. I had also become friends with the buyers, having lived next to them for 1 year and 11 months. Lois thought the seller should make the repairs but the sellers are under no obligation to do anything. Lois and Ben could buy the house and make their own repairs in order to get a mortgage, or **vacate!**

Each asked my opinion. I put them in contact with a

real estate attorney who charged them $500 and worked up a compromise. The sellers made a few of the repairs and paid for the material for Ben to make the other repairs from the labor end. Lois had her baby, they own the house, and everything worked out.

Solution

It's far better to **avoid** problems than it is to handle them once they arise. The decision to purchase should have been made months **before** the deadline which would have given Ben and Lois time to look for another residence and not automatically vault the owner into such a command position.

A Realtor should have handled the entire transaction from the beginning. I think the telephone bills between here and another city 400 miles away between owner and buyer added up to what the Realtors commission would have been.

The principals argued for over two months—long distance. The cost of gallons of *Pepto Bismol* for four sets of upset stomachs, trips to the chiropractor to relieve the tension, and the unkind thoughts each had towards the other was simply not worth it.

So, who should **not** own a home?

a.   Those who have a lifestyle where their time is completely taken up.

b.   Those who hate painting, cutting grass or fixing things.

c.   Those who enjoy apartment, condo or high-rise living where maintenance is taken care of.

d.   Those who never can keep a steady job.

e.   The elderly who are not physically capable of doing home maintenance.

Owning a home takes **time, work,** and **expense!** Either you like cutting grass, occasional painting, sweeping, working with plants and flowers, washing windows, checking the air conditioner drip pan, lighting the pilot light, fixing a faucet leak or you don't. There are dozens of "little things" that can go wrong or need checking almost weekly and if you can't do **some** repair work, lease for the rest of your life.

> And **don't** buy a home at a time of a *big boom* because **after** the boom, there's a bust. The prices are inflated and/or the interest rates are high.

But, if you strive for the American Dream with having kids, a suburban, a dog, lawn mower and the feeling of having something, owning is the only way to do all of these things. To me, it's a great feeling. Again, *Different strokes for different folks.* Some people don't want homes and thus, shouldn't have them.

If you are **thinking** of buying a home, take this test to see if the timing and your particular situation is right. If you mark mostly affirmative answers, buy a house!

1.   I have money in savings that is drawing minimal interest. I can build equity in a house, can't I?

2.   I am tired of paying rent and seeing my payments going up in smoke. It's smart to own, isn't it?

3.   My apartment complex is fully occupied and the owners are starting to refurbish, and I think the rent will go up soon. I can own a house for what I'm paying, right?

4.   I'm getting periodic raises at work so I'm earning more money than ever before. I can afford a house.

5.   I'd like to get a dog, but not only do these rental rules not allow it, it would be unfair to keep a dog cooped up in an apartment all day.

6.   I'd like to put a swing or hammock on my patio but I know I'm not allowed. I can't paint my apartment a different color either. Rules.

7.   Chances are I'll find some unlucky girl who consents to marry me in the coming months. If I get a house now, I can pick out what I like!

8.   I think I would have fun cutting grass and planting flowers. It's time I got a taste of "getting back to nature". And, like Tom Tynan, I think I would enjoy that

feeling of permanency, stability, owning something, having control.

I'm going to stop here before I get absolutely ludicrous but, you get the idea. Now, that you have decided to buy a home, do it the smart way. I suggest you consider . . .

Chapter 2

WORKING WITH A REALTOR

I'd like to list a few titles that I feel are useful for both buyer and seller. I'll begin with the term . . .

REAL ESTATE AGENT

To become a licensed real estate AGENT (in Texas for example) a person needs to complete 180 classroom hours of post-secondary education and must pass the Agent's Real Estate Examination to be licensed. They also need at least 30 additional classroom hours each year for three years after they **are** licensed.

REALTOR

A REALTOR, must first become a real estate agent by passing the state examination and be licensed to sell real property. Whereas, to bear the title of **Realtor**, a person must still pass the state test to become licensed, but is also a member in good standing with the **National Association of Realtors,** an organization with a strict code of ethics set out by their state and local boards.

REAL ESTATE BROKER

A BROKER'S license requires **900** classroom hours and at least two years of active real estate experience as an agent. There are also Mandatory Continuing Education requirements that apply throughout each licensee's career.

The fastest and most efficient way to find the home you want is through a Realtor (real estate agent or broker). These people are in the business of finding the right home for you and spend their time researching and learning things that will make your house-shopping easier.

Find a Realtor who has access to a **MLS (Multiple Listing Service)** that have a **computerized** list of photos and information on just about every home for sale on the market. By working with a computer they can show you numerous homes with complete information on each. In a matter of minutes you can look at a home and get enough information to eliminate it and move on to the next.

When you decide on a house, the agent accepts whatever you offer and is obligated to present it to the Seller. Their knowledge often helps consummate the deal.

If everything is settled (and you haven't **pre-qualified** for a loan), agents know where to **direct** you to find a mortgage company. They are not allowed to give you the name of **an** inspector or **a** mortgage company but they can furnish you with a list from which you might choose. They direct you from start to finish. For first-time home buyers, a good Realtor is a Godsend!

Of course it's the bright way to house-shop. Qualified Realtors know **all** the answers about their respective neighborhoods. If they're good Realtors they have walked through each home they plan to show you. Once they know what you're looking for, they are able to eliminate the homes that you don't want. They can tell you about a particular neighborhood, about schools, public transportation, golf courses, malls, distance to a freeway, **(even some dirt about the neighbors).**

KNOW WHAT YOU WANT

I contacted several real estate agents who concurred on their biggest gripe; people don't often tell them the **truth** about the price home they can realistically afford. Their second "problem area" was that many people don't know **what** they want. But, that's okay because the agent's job is to find the home for you—once **you** determine what it is.

No matter how adamant you are on what you want, you'll change your mind. It happens to almost everybody when they look at the pictures on that MLS computer screen; you see something that looks so appealing you change your mind. Hey! We're human, and we're allowed that prerogative!

Before you contact an agent, sit down with your spouse and decide three basic things:

1.   The **PRICE** home you can **realistically** afford.

2.   The **SIZE** of the home you need; 2 bedroom, 3 bedroom, 2 or 3 baths.

3.   The **LOCATION**; the area of the city where you **think** you'd like to live.

PRICE

It's a waste of time to ask an agent to look for a home in the $200,000 price range when all you can afford is $100,000. Don't worry about **impressing** the agent, all they want to do is sell you a house.

In determining the price, make certain you're aware of what that means. First-time home buyers figure if they get a home that sells for $100,000 over 30 years, that it comes out to be $3333.33 divided by 12 months and the payment will be $277.78 per month. Hardly!

Mortgage mathematics differs from the arithmetic we learned back in grade school; it works by an amortization scale that includes the interest. Here's an example:

Let's say you want to buy a home for $100,000. The interest rate is, say 8%. If you go for the standard 30-year loan, your monthly payment will be $734. A 25-year loan will be $836 and a 15-year loan would cost you $956 per month.

Now, that's repayment of the loan **only!** You still have to find out from your realtor what the **taxes** and **insurance** are for that home. Discouraged? What I often wonder (and I'll bet you do too) is what kind of business are those people in who own these $200,000 and $300,000 and up, homes?

SIZE

This doesn't mean total square footage. Agents aren't allowed to quote or list a home this way. Your primary request should be the number of **bedrooms** you need. **You** measure when you're walking through the house.

Yes, bring along a tape measure that is at least 25 feet long. Have the agent hold the "dumb" end and you measure the rooms and mark them on that pad I asked you to carry.

Next, is how many bathrooms you need, mostly depending on how many children you have (or plan) and their gender and age? If you have one teenage boy and one teenage girl and aren't completely broke from doctor bills, clothes, schools, summer camps, weekly allowances and a car for each, try to find a home with **three** bathrooms.

> How in the world did the Walton's do it? All those kids, mom, dad, grandma and grandpa and **one** bathroom.

Along with the number of bedrooms and baths, you'll want to find a home in your price range with a two or three-car garage, at least a two-car and carport. Now, who gets the garage, who gets the carport and whose car will be in the weather? Well, than can be handled by who leaves home first in the morning, huh? Then maybe not? Maybe it's who has the most expensive car?

Anyway, work that out later, **after** you get the house. I've heard of people who had knock-down, drag-out fights in the Realtor's office over who gets which garage and which space. Don't you do that, please!

With the number of bedrooms and bathrooms decided upon, now give the Realtor a general idea on the amount of rooms you'd like such as a dining room, large den (preferably with a fireplace) breakfast room, formal living room (who has those anymore?)and maybe a library or smaller room to be used as an office. Remember, these extra rooms mean a higher price so don't forget those monthly payments.

LOCATION

Again, what are your priorities? Closer to his work or hers? Closer to schools or work? Is there a school bus that passes in your neighborhood? What about the **schools** in that area? Do you want to live in a subdivision? Want a big lot? Want to live near a major thruway? In an isolated area or close to the city? Is a large supermarket, close by, a necessity or is a small convenience store a few blocks away okay?

Must there be restaurants or movies close to where you live or do you mind the drive? How about a shopping mall? Does the neighborhood have a maintenance fund? A crime watch? Is the street wide enough? Is parking allowed on the street except for parties or weekend visits by relatives? Your Realtor knows the answers to **all** of these questions. That's why it's so important to get . . .

THE RIGHT AGENT

Just as with every other profession, there are "good" agents and there are "not-so-good" agents. If you don't know any agents, call a company and talk with an agent. Tell them you want to buy a house. Tell them what you want and then . . .

Give them some time to research their inventory and print out a list of homes. Then, make an appointment to visit them to look at what they have. A good agent will have a print-out of homes in your price range and location listed on their computer for you to peruse and eliminate the majority with a quick look.

Then, they'll get down to the finer points and look for the other criteria like size of the yard, one, two or three-car garage, size of den, fireplace, carpeted (including color), hardwood or tiled floors, swimming pool, patio, deck, spa, big trees, landscaping, what else is in the area other than close proximity to work and is there another area that's "almost" as close that you like better and can afford. And, Oh yes! The **style** of the house. Do you like old english, contemporary, country?

From the computer information and from listening to your comments on what you've perhaps looked at, need and/or want, the agent will be able to narrow it down even more. All of this can be done without leaving the agent's office. Then the work begins for both you and the agent; you start **looking** at these homes.

One agent I spoke with works with 6 or 7 homes in a certain location on computer then takes their client for a drive. If you like the neighborhood, continue to look and if not, get back to the computer. The computer shows pictures of the homes and the number of rooms, etc., but it doesn't show the neighborhood!

Don't be embarrassed at the time it takes; agents are trained not to appear aggravated even if they are about to "bust a gut". Also, this is a large investment and where you'll spend the majority of your life so take time in choosing and get **exactly** what you want.

One agent I spoke with drives their clients to the best home first. "By looking at the best first," the agent said, "they merely look briefly at the others and we go back to the original one. It cuts my time by more than half and I get the people what they want and I get started with the contract." Still another takes the prospective buyer to the worst one first.

I don't know which method is best for the agent but for **you,** look at them all! Try to establish some rapport with the agent and talk to them as a friend and sort of partner. Tell them what you like, and as you and the agent walk through some of the places the agent will pick up more on what you like just by listening to your comments.

If you don't feel comfortable with your agent, **get another one!** Then another, until you find one you feel you can work with. You owe **no allegiance** to a Realtor and you may choose another one at any time.

If you are working with a Realtor and tell anyone you are, Realtor is pronounced REAL-TOR, just like it's spelled. Many people put an "i" someplace in there and say "REAL-**IT**-TOR. It's the same as the word ATHLETE, pronounced ATH-LETE, not ATH-**UH**-LETE. See! I've got me some learnin'.

Here's some additional information I **copied** verbatim from a form promulgated by the Texas Real Estate Commission. I know that the state of California has a similar form; I don't know about other states. Ask your broker about it.

This form gives information on your Realtor (broker or agent) to those **buying,** and also to those **selling** a home. It concerns your broker (Realtor or agent) if they both list **and** attempt to sell the house.

INFORMATION AND DISCLOSURE REGARDING REAL ESTATE AGENCY RELATIONS (FORM)

WHO WILL THE BROKER REPRESENT IN THIS TRANSACTION

*Before working with a real estate broker you should know that the duties of the broker to you depend upon whom the broker represents. If you are a prospective seller (landlord or owner) or a prospective buyer, you should know that the broker who lists the property for sale or lease is the **Owner's** agent. A broker who acts as subagent represents the Owner through the listing broker, whereas a broker who represents the **Buyer's agent** represents the **Buyer**. A broker may not represent both an Owner **and** a Buyer in the same transaction **unless** both Owner and Buyer consent, in writing, to this representation. A broker can assist in locating a property, preparing a contract or lease, or obtain financing without representing you. Brokers are obligated, by law, to treat you honestly and fairly.*

WHAT ARE THE BROKER'S DUTIES TO YOU

*If the broker represents the owner (seller): The broker typically becomes the **owner's agent** by entering into a listing agreement with the owner or by agreeing to act as a subagent through a listing broker. A subagent may work in a different real estate office. A listing agent or subagent can **assist** the buyer but, in essence, **does not** represent the buyer. A listing agent or subagent must place the interest of* *the owner first. The buyer should not tell a listing agent or subagent anything the buyer would not want the owner to know, because a listing agent or subagent may disclose to the Owner any material information they find out.*

This part says that the agent can tell a **secret** they learn from the buyer and may tattle back to the owner. If the Buyer says, "I really want this house and I need to move in two weeks or goblins will get me", the agent can run to the owner and say, "Don't make any deals. This buyer is desperate!"

Conversely, if the broker represents the **buyer,** the broker typically becomes the **buyer's agent**. I personally, see no problem with an agent that both lists **and** sells a house. I would think they have better rapport with the seller and could convey whatever message or offer that is made.

If you like your broker, agent or Realtor, if you believe in them, if you feel they are fair, I'd think it would work better for you.

What they're saying is . . .

1.   A buyer's agent can *assist* the owner but does not **represent** the owner.

2.   A buyer's agent must place the interest of the buyer **first!** The seller should not tell the buyer's agent anything they would not want the buyer to know, because a **buyer's agent** must disclose to the buyer any material

information he or she knows.

The above statement is the same as the other only the parties are switched. Like Joe Garrigola said, "*Six of this and a Dozen of that!*" Or something to that effect. It isn't funny, it doesn't make sense, but neither does all of this writing. Yet, it must be a major problem or there wouldn't be such a form.

IF THE BROKER REPRESENTS BOTH

*A broker may **not** act as an agent for more than one party to a transaction unless the broker complies with specific requirements established by law. In addition to providing the parties with this form, **the broker must enter into a written agreement with each party** (Didn't it already state this in a paragraph up above? Hey, I'm copying it word-for word. I hope it helps you.) which authorizes the broker to represent more than one party and sets forth who will pay the broker's fee. The broker is required to treat both parties honestly and impartially so as not to favor one party or work to the disadvantage of any party. Unless written permission from the appropriate party is obtained, the broker is prohibited from disclosing:*

*(a)   That the seller will accept a price **less than** the asking price.*

*(b)   That the buyer will pay a price **greater than** the price submitted in a written offer.*

*(c)   **Any** confidential information.*

*(d)   Any other information a party specifically instructs the broker in writing **not** to disclose, unless disclosure is required by law.*

The broker's duties are more limited if he or she represents both parties. There are potential conflicts-of-interest when a broker represents more than one party. The broker is obligated to inform each party of all facts the broker knows which would affect the party's decision to permit the broker to represent both the seller and the buyer. For example, the broker would inform the seller if the broker expects to represent the buyer in purchasing additional properties in the near future.

Whew! No wonder people hate lawyers. A full, single-spaced page form with all this *mumbo-jumbo* on it discourages buyers and sellers, don't you think? In deference to attorneys, people hate them until they need their help if they're being sued, to help in suing or to save their life when accused of murder.

It's the same with this form. Because of human greed or misunderstanding, there had been scores of problems when an agent both **took a listing** on property, then **sold** the property. Thus, this seemingly dumb form became necessary. It's called dotting your "*i*'s" and crossing your "*t*'s".

If you choose to have a broker represent you, you should enter into a written contract that clearly establishes the obligations of both you and the broker and that sets out how and by whom your broker will be paid. You have the right to choose the type of representation you wish to receive. Payment of a fee to a broker does not necessarily establish that the broker represents you. If you have any questions regarding the duties and responsibilities of the broker, you should resolve those questions before going further. Regardless of the agency relationships which may be established, you have the responsibility to protect your own interests. Once you have read and discussed this information with the broker, please acknowledge receipt of a copy of this form. Your cooperation will help the broker to comply with the rules of the Texas Real Estate Commission. The broker is required to provide this form to you and disclose below who the broker represents. This form is used in residential, commercial and other types of real estate transactions.

What one part of this form tells, is that if you own a house and a broker comes to you for a listing, they represent you! If they, personally or through a subagent, attempt to sell your house to a prospective buyer, they are **obligated** (by being your representative) to give you any tidbits of information that will help you get what you want. The second part says the same but is in the **buyer's** favor.

The big kicker is if they do both list and attempt to sell the property, they have to get this form filled out by each of you, a CYA measure, (cover your . . . something or other.

Chapter 3

HOW TO SECURE FINANCING

In order to get you the most accurate, up-to-date information, I've reserved this chapter for Paula Ginsburg, senior loan officer at First Financial Mortgage Corporation. I've dealt with Paula, I like her and I trust her knowledge.

I am a builder and feel, unashamedly so, that I am as good as any. I know about building and I know about products and equipment to build but my expertise in financing is not expert.

I asked a few questions then decided it was best to just have Paula talk about the various loans. You see, as proud as I am over my knowledge of building, I yield to experts in other fields. Besides, it's easier than writing all of this myself. So, I asked Paula the first question most people need to know. And that is . . .

Q.   How does a person find a mortgage company?

A.   Mortgage people are competitive. There are many mortgage companies willing to make loans and they'll cut rates and make special deals. Read the newspaper, check the yellow pages, listen to the radio (KTRH has companies who advertise) and **check the rates!** There's no need to see if the company is listed in Dun and Bradstreet or the New York Stock Exchange. If they are willing to loan you money and you like the terms, go for it!

Q.   Assuming your company is competitive, tell me

what benefit they offer a home buyer that they can't find at any other company?

A.   My company is unique. When I first became loan officer I worked with one investor for seven years. But now, we broker to maybe 40 or 50 different investors. Let's get technical for a moment.

Mortgage rates are dictated through the activity of the bond market. We call it the *secondary market.* Buying and selling bonds determines the current mortgage rate. To call around for the best price is no longer necessary if you find a company who has multiple investors, such as mine.

Q.   What are some of the questions a borrower needs to ask when talking to a mortgage company?

A.   They need to ask several key questions, such as . . .

1.   What are the going rates on mortgages?
2.   Do you deal with multiple investors?
3.   Do you offer a float down?
4.   What are your closing costs?

They should be writing all of this down so they can . . .

COMPARE RATES

Ask how long the rate the mortgage company quotes is good for if you "lock it in" today? For instance, I can *lock in a rate* (guarantee it) for a person simply by talking to them on the telephone but I would like to have them come in the next day or two to fill out an application and sign it.

If I lock in a person to a rate and the rate **lessens** before I send in the necessary paperwork, I'll give them the lower rate. If the rate **increases** during this same time span, they are locked in.

MULTIPLE INVESTORS

That's why having multiple investors makes it easier to change investors to suit the borrower. I had a person with a fine loan package and gave them a rate by my primary investor. When the borrower found a place to buy, the investor I submitted it to balked when the words "high rise condo" entered.

But, having the luxury of dealing with **multiple** investors, without alarming the borrower, I went through my file of investors and found the same rate for them with another investor. Nobody really cares **who** is lending the money, only that the money spends.

By "investors" I don't mean only individuals but rather large companies like banks, lending institutions or large corporations. These groups have loan personnel working for them who look over who, how much, how long, and on what they are lending.

FLOAT DOWNS

Some people use the term "float down" rate which

means you have a **one-time** ability to float down to a lower rate. Lending companies with but one investor can't offer this; you're locked in and what you are quoted at the time you signed the application is what you get even if the loan rate drops a full percentage point or more.

This means you have but **one chance** to get a lower rate before you **close** into a mortgage. Look at the fluctuation in rates on a daily basis and when it gets good, go with it. It's sort of a little game you play, like the stock market. If the rate goes up you stay with the original rate you locked in with. If the rate goes down, you have that **single opportunity** to "float down" to a lower rate. If it goes down even **lower**, too bad. You made your choice and have to stick with it.

If the interest rate is 8%, a gross income of $30,000 is sufficient to qualify for an $85,000 mortgage, providing you don't have a high debt-burden like up to the limit on a few credit cards, big furniture payment, paying for a boat, a truck, and an automobile. Your mortgage payment would be $595 per month not including taxes and insurance. Don't forget utilities!

CLOSING COSTS

Closing costs of these loans should be almost standard and I'd like potential borrowers to talk about this. A loan origination fee is usually 1% which is industry-wide standard and the only fee that goes to the mortgage company.

Additional closing costs can be required to place in escrow which include 2 or 3 months of prepaid taxes, PMI (Prepaid Mortgage Insurance), a one year paid up homeowners insurance policy (which they call hazard insurance), and other expenses.

Closing costs are negotiable with the seller. Some buyers ask the seller to go **up** on the price of the property. This enables them to borrow more from the mortgage company and the buyer and seller can work together on this. It's done often.

TYPES OF MORTGAGES

ARMS (Adjustable Rate Mortgages)

These are for people whom we know will have a **rise** in income during the coming years. For instance, a college graduate who is beginning a job where we know their pay will increase. Maybe a graduate doctor or attorney who will make more as their practice builds. Or a young executive who will surely get a raise in income or, for those who are going to live in this home only 3 to 5 years at the most.

Also, for those who own a home and want to buy a second home before they sell the first. When they do sell the first home they can put that money toward their present mortgage thereby lowering the amount they borrowed on their new home.

Adjustable mortgages give you a rate that will **not fluctuate** more than 2% per year. Contrary to the loans in the mid 1980's, these loans now have a cap; we run the numbers and see what the highest payment will ever be.

Another situation is if a homeowner has their home for sale and qualifies for **two payments** but have no idea how long it will take to sell their former house. When they do sell, if they have a **conventional loan** they can plunk down a lot of cash to reduce the number of **years** they have to pay on their new home, but the payments remain the same.

On an **Adjustable Rate Mortgage,** if they put down a lot of cash, the **numbers are redone** and it **lowers the amount** of the monthly payments! See the difference?

15 and 30-year Fixed-rate Mortgage

These are for people who are on a fixed income or for those whose job warrants periodic raises to cover **only** the rise in cost-of-living. These are the folks who make out a monthly budget and they have to follow this budget. Or, the very conservative person who resists change; they want to know what they are obligated to pay without surprises. This type of loan is also for retired people (again with a fixed income) who are on social security and/or living from savings.

These mortgages are exactly what the name implies; **Fixed Rate.** The payment remains the same for the length of the loan. You may, if you choose, pay more, thereby paying for your home faster. For instance, let's say you are paying $500 a month on a 30-year mortgage.

If you pay but **one additional** note per year (a 13th payment), you can, by making this **one extra payment per year,** reduce the year payout on your home from 30 years down maybe 16 or 17 years. Be certain to **ask** your loan officer about this and get the exact time on your particular mortgage if you chose to make this 13th payment.

5-25 and 7-23 Fixed-rate Mortgages

These are the new type of mortgages that were created "for the times". They are designed for those who plan to be in a home for 5 to 7 years such as those beginning professionals whose income is almost **guaranteed** to rise dramatically. It enables them to **immediately** occupy a nice home with lower payments for these "business-building" years.

It differs from the **ARMS** mortgage in that they are **fixed rates** for the first 5 (or 7) years and will not go neither up nor down during these 5 or 7 beginning years. Then, the payment adjusts **(goes up)** to a fixed rate. By then, if things go as planned, they can afford it.

If, during this time, the rates are lowered, they can always **refinance** or sell and move to an even finer residence. Interest rates fell drastically in the early 90's and there was a flood of people in daily to buy, build and/or refinance to this lower rate.

QUALIFYING FOR THE MORTGAGE

There are two ways to do this. One is by **pre-qualifying** for a loan and two, is **filling out an application.** I'll walk you through the steps, lengthy as they may seem.

Step #1 Pre-qualifying

If you are planning to look for a property in the next month or two, you can **pre-qualify** for a mortgage. Maybe your job location is going to change and you want to move closer to your work. Perhaps the kids are grown and married (and moved) and you want to move into a smaller place. Or your lease is up and you want to entertain the thought of buying instead of renting. It isn't necessary that you have even **selected** a home to buy, only that you **plan** to and you'd like to know what price home you can qualify for.

The rule is, the amount of money you can qualify for can be **equal to** but not **greater than** 28% of your gross monthly income. You can purchase any home you choose (depending on the down payment) but the total monthly note is determined by this gross-income percentage. This 28% does not include utility bills or health club membership, but it does include larger bills such as car notes, bank loans or monthly charge card bills.

Even though I talk about standard rules, there are exceptions to those rules. For instance, if a borrower comes in for this pre-approval, should something show up on their credit that they can explain or clear up, it gives them and the lender the opportunity to get it worked out.

Pre-qualifying is the smart way to go. It saves time and shattered dreams because it tells the home buyer what they can comfortably afford and not have them go into neighborhoods or houses that seem idyllic and then discover that they are not within their budget.

Q.   How about a down payment? How much does a person need?

A.   The former standard was 20% minimum, but with today's "creative financing" you can put down as little as 10%, in some cases only 5%. If a person has good credit and a stable job history and their income warrants it, they can get in with 5% down."

If you need a **larger** down payment than you anticipated, nearly one third of all first-time home buyers **borrow it** from relatives or friends. Borrow from or against a profit-sharing plan at work, or borrow against an insurance policy. Chances are you'll get a better rate than from banks. Sell the boat, cancel your $1000-a-year deer lease, sell some *crappola* you've been saving and never use or win the lottery. The fact is, if you want this home badly enough you'll **find** that down payment.

Step #2 Filling out an Application

Somehow or other you have the down payment and now you make a physical appearance at your mortgage company to fill out a loan application. These are the items you'll need to bring with you.

a.   W-2 forms for the last 2 years.

b.   2 current pay stubs from your most recent paychecks. If both husband and wife are working, you bring 2 from each.

c.   Name, address and account numbers of any **long-term** debts like a beach house, large boat, auto.

d.   If you recently sold your home and you're now renting, bring a copy of that closing statement and the name and address of your landlord.

e.   Three months of statements on your assets such as checking and saving accounts, brokerage account, retirement, thrift, IRA's, C.D's, trust fund . . . everything that is liquid. List cash value of life insurance, annuities, everything and anything that is an asset, even if you can't get to it right away. Anything that shows your history of saving or investing money will help.

Each loan package is different. There is no *standard* loan. I've had people who made enormous amounts of money but hadn't saved a dime and have poor credit. Of course I'd take a person who earned less but who was stable. The "numbers" so to speak, take a common sense approach and with this information, we can make an educated judgment call. We listen to stories but we like the numbers.

The cost of a getting a pre-approval amount is the cost of the credit report the mortgage company has to pay for after taking your application. Normal charges range between $75 and $100.

Step #3 Find the Property

After you find the property you'd like to buy and you've signed an agreement with the seller or seller's agent, you will have to come up with Approximately $300 for the appraisal of this property. To determine what your out-of-pocket expense might be, the following list should help you in determining your closing costs.

Step #4 Closing Costs

Different mortgage lenders and different states vary on rules and practices of who pays what—buyer or seller. And don't be alarmed at this long list because it is filled out by the title company and you'll see it **before** you are obligated to pay whatever your share might be.

Earnest Money Deposit
Interest points charged by lender
Loan assumption fee
Loan origination or discount fee
Prepaid mortgage insurance
Credit report
Appraisal
Property survey
Initial mortgage payment
Payment for inspections of property
Recording fees
Prepaid homeowner's insurance first year
Prorated property taxes
Attorney's fees
Title search/or policy including insurance
State and local closing taxes and fees
Down payment (less earnest money
     already paid)
Prorated maintenance for remainder of
     month
Other closing costs
Amount needed at closing

Again, don't let all of these items frighten you; it's only part of buying a home and everybody does it. Talk to your mortgage lender about this list before you get too involved. They will be able to tell you approximately how much money you will need.

We are coming along nicely and, **you're approved,** you and the seller have a **signed agreement**, and you're ready to close. Make certain you have . . .

1. A cashiers check for the down payment.
2. Arranged for homeowner's insurance through your agent.
3. Had your property surveyed or have a copy of the survey the mortgage lender had made.
4. Made a final walk-thru.
5. Have had your closing costs explained by the title company or your attorney.
6. The deed recorded after closing.

Much of this will have been explained in detail to you by the title company or loan officer. **But**, if there is something you don't understand, **ask!** And have it explained again and again until you do understand. Don't be over-anxious to purchase anything of this magnitude and let things *slip by.*

OTHER OPTIONS FOR MORTGAGE LOANS

Other than a Conventional loan there are FHA and VA loans.

FHA LOANS

Anyone may apply. Maximum ratios are 29% of your gross monthly income for housing expenses and 41% for the total debt. The attractive part of an FHA loan is that the down payment may be as little as 3% and you can **borrow** that, legally! Also, some of the closing costs can be financed as part of the mortgage loan, and the seller **may** pay the discount points.

Fixed-rate and adjustable-rate mortgages are available. **Mortgage insurance** is required and it may be paid as a one-time premium at closing or the premiums can be **included** in the monthly payments for the run of the loan.

Maximum FHA loan amounts are governed to local median priced homes and differ in various states. The maximum for Houston, Texas, for example is $101,500. Dallas is a bit higher. The loan amounts not only vary from state to state, but from **city** to **city**! Get this information from your realtor!

VA LOANS

Veterans and/or reservists who have 90 days wartime or 180 peacetime service are eligible if they didn't receive a Dishonorable Discharge. Unmarried, surviving spouses of veterans who died from service-related illness or injury are eligible also. Call your local VA office for information and a brochure or ask your real estate agent.

The maximum qualifying ratio is 41% of gross monthly income for total debt, including housing expenses. A qualifying veteran (or unmarried surviving spouse) can apply with **no down payment!** The veteran must pay a "funding fee" of 1.25 % and allowable closing costs. Fees to the veterans are controlled and both **fixed-rate** and **adjustable-rate mortgages** are available. **No mortgage insurance is required!**

FHA, VA and Conventional loans account for the majority of mortgage loans in the United States, although "creative financing" such as owner financing is also a possibility. Your Realtor can explain this in detail; ask them! Each type of loan has its restrictions, which may be offset by its advantages.

With an **FHA loan**, you are limited to the amount of the loan but your chances of qualifying are easier. The low down payments and being able to finance closing costs means you won't need much up-front money, certainly an attractive feature.

With a **Conventional loan,** you'll have to meet more stringent requirements plus you'll need a down payment and closing costs, but you can borrow more and have a larger range of financing plans. Many people, especially those who made a profit from selling their former home, might choose to make a down payment for tax reasons. Or, to lower the monthly payments.

The **VA loan** offers generous terms to veterans. They deserve a break, don't you think?

Chapter 4

HOW TO REALLY LOOK FOR A HOME

LOCATION—COST—MINIMUM REQUIREMENTS

LOCATION

In smaller towns this might not be as difficult as in a city the size of New York, Los Angeles, Chicago, Houston or Miami—any city with a population over a million. These cities are spread out to where there are actually different cities within the city.

The first thing I advise people to do if they are new in town is to contact one of the large real estate firms and get whatever information they can from them. These people are "in the business" and if you tell them what you want, they will find it for you.

I spoke with a real estate relocator in Austin, Texas last week and he told me about one couple facing a dilemma. She was being transferred from another city so she wanted to find a place near her job. He wanted a mountain view.

The problem was that her job location was on **flat land** and his mountains were many miles away. They had to decide who wanted what the most and which was most important. There was no way to please both. The end result was they bought a giant mural of mountain scenery to paste on their sliding glass window and settled for the flat land that was closer to her work.

At one time it was wise to rent for several months to get the "feel" of the city. But with these computers, a Realtor can pinpoint a location for you in minutes. Call a real estate agent and cut down on your expense and time.

If you're being moved by your company, they will supply you with all the information through their relocation service. But it's different for those who have to haul whatever they can stack in a borrowed truck and in their van, pulling a trailer after most of the "big stuff" was sold in a "Moving Sale" for ten cents on a dollar.

You've seen it—perhaps you've done it. Husband driving the truck with 9-year old Skippy needing to go to the bathroom every 10 miles and baby Jennifer riding with mom in the van (crying for any number of reasons) is an experience humans shouldn't have to suffer.

If you're moving to look for work, there's little choice. Usually one of the adults goes to the new town a few weeks or so ahead of time and tries to find a place to move directly in to. It's expensive to rent a motel and look together, with furniture getting rained on, the cost of storing prohibiting long searches, not to mention the squalling children. This is when a fast, competent Realtor is appreciated.

The procedure is the same in each instance:

1.   Find a real estate agent or agency.

2.   Tell them what you're looking for.
3.   Tell them what you can afford.
4.   Ask about various areas in the city or tell them the area (if you know) where to look.
5.   Get busy and look as quickly and as efficiently as you can.

You might not find **exactly** what you want in the time you have. If not, it's wise to move into an apartment for several months rather than move into a neighborhood you haven't researched or into a home that you haven't completely checked out.

COST

What I would like you to do is **look wisely** and don't buy until you've checked everything out. Far too often people strap themselves down to payments they simply can't afford and if you can "barely" afford it, look for something a little less expensive. You know me, I look for things to break or that need to be replaced.

Whatever the basic cost of your home is, don't forget to add the cost of air conditioning, heat, water, garbage pick-up, cable television, taxes, homeowners insurance, gardening tools, lawn maintenance and things that need fixing or replacing.

Again, please don't "big time" the agent on price. Don't tell them you want a home for $200,000 when you can only afford, and qualify for, a home that is worth $100,000. You might **want** a home for $200,000 but don't waste the agent's time or yours by being unrealistic. Besides, if you look at a few homes that you **can't** afford, you'll never be satisfied with what you **can** afford. Far too many people do this.

MINIMUM REQUIREMENTS

In **really** looking for a new home and assuming you've already given the information I mention earlier in this book to an agent, all you need to do now is look at a lot of houses. You have the price homes you are looking for, you have a general area where you think you'd like to live, now, let's look at the home itself from all angles.

First, just **drive-by** the homes that looked good on paper and start your process of elimination. If it isn't to your liking on the outside, chances are it won't be to your liking on the inside.

If your Realtor has been inside this home and if they have your list of wants, they'll point out that this particular home that might not look so great on the drive-by has a walk-in pantry, sunken tub, a wine cellar, bomb shelter, mirror on the bedroom ceiling (whatever turns you on) and you'll stop and look and maybe decide the outside isn't so bad after all.

SCREENING THE HOMES

If you find a home that looks good as you drive by it, back up, stop, get out of the car and stand in front and look. Look for as long as you want and if there are things that just don't "click" with you, there's no reason to go inside. Don't waste your time.

When you have it narrowed down to a few homes, go have lunch and discuss it privately then come back to the ones that make you **all** happy. There are such homes.

Look at the "big picture" when searching for a home, some of which I mentioned earlier; the location, other houses, next-door neighbors, the yard, garage, the general look of the home. In your screening process . . .

Look for ugly telephone poles, giant phone lines in the back, and easements that stick up with all sorts of boxes and lines running along your property.

Ask the Realtor about any drainage problems. Is there an apartment building next door where you have noise and loud music playing all the time? Ask questions about anything that might cause you unpleasantness. **Ask now! Once you move in, it will be too late!**

How about the size of the yard? Do you have one child or three? Is there room in the yard for a swing? A sandbox? A dog kennel? A swimming pool? If there's a lot of grass? Who cuts it? Do **you** have the time to do it? Can you afford a yardman? Do you even **want** grass?

SCREENING THE NEIGHBORHOOD (AND THE NEIGHBORS)

If the neighborhood is to your liking, what about your

next-door neighbors? Do they seem nice? Are their kids reasonably sane or do you have to plan on a 10-foot fence or start throwing *Miracle Gro* on those slow-growing hedges to get them up to 15 feet to block that old car that's being constantly worked on?

Do they have dogs? Do the dogs bark at all hours? Will their Pit Bulls just permanently cripple or simply **devour** your Pomeranian?

In every neighborhood with kids, there will be arguments. Small children will make comparisons like, Who's mommy is the prettiest? Who's daddy is the strongest? And, who's house is the biggest? If **your** child comes across this, the perfect solution is . . . for the child to say nothing and walk away.

When the offending child asks where they're going, have your child reply. "I'm going home to my **ugly** mommy and **wimpy** daddy to our house that is **smaller** than yours.

Since it is so small, we saved money on the amount of insulation, on the mortgage, on the paint and on maid service. Because of this savings we're going on a two-week vacation to **Disney World!** See you when I get back.

Now, who says I don't have a sense of humor and that my jokes aren't funny?

I know it's tiring but I promise you, it's worth the time and effort. Look at **all** the homes on the computer that **might** be what you like and can afford, then take that drive-by. Perhaps you and your Realtor will find what you want after looking at but a few.

Usually, there won't be **hundreds** of homes that meet your criteria as far as size, location and price anyway. Remember, make that list of what you want—that you can comfortably afford—then follow this procedure. You won't go wrong. Now, let's take what I call "the closer look".

A CLOSER LOOK

Once you find two or three houses that seem to be what you wouldn't mind living in, it's time for a **closer** look.

Start off with house number one and walk around the *outside* of the house; don't even go inside. Ask your Realtor to walk with you or do it alone and let the Realtor talk to the owner, assuming the house is occupied.

Look at the fence, over the fence into your neighbor's yard, take a closer look at the roof and keep an eye peeled for rotting wood that you couldn't detect on the drive-by look. If you find something that turns you off, tell your Realtor it isn't necessary to even go inside. **Don't waste time!**

Let's say the outside passes your inspection. While you were looking over the fence into your neighbor's yard you saw them watering the grass or tending the flower beds and they said "hello" and smiled at you. This stuff counts. So the next step is to go **inside!**

If the home is occupied, it's more difficult to see how "your" things will fit but take a minute or two in each room and try to *imagine* where you'd put this or that and how it **might** look. Look at the carpet, the closets, the windows, the size of the rooms, and ignore the paint or wallpaper. If it's not to your liking, these are easy to change.

Try to make this "look-thru" on your own. A smart Realtor will allow this. Not that a trained Realtor would yap in your ear and not give you time to look, you want to take your time and "place" your furniture in various rooms—and only you know how to do this.

Now, try to picture yourself **living in** this house, in each room, doing what you want. Does that make sense to you? Imagine what you would do to change or to add, to make it the way you'd like.

And, **don't** be "taken in" by the *fluff*. I don't have anything against crown molding but I want you to look at the basics, to deal with this academically, to look at each room as a three-dimensional box.

Will it be large enough for you and your family? How about the den? Will the big couch and two recliners fit into it? Is it easy to get to the kitchen and come from the kitchen with snacks? Can you just lean over the service bar and hand stuff to the lazy occupants who usually inhabit this area, you know, the spot just in front of the large-screen TV?

Do the same with each bedroom and bath, with the closets, entry from the garage, laundry room, pantry, and the areas that you use most of the time.

Is the height of the ceilings satisfactory? Do you have two vanities in your bath area with only one wash basin and you know you'll need two? Are both closets the same size? If not, who gets the bigger one? Is there a bathtub and shower or is it a bathtub/shower? Look for the things that are most important to you!

If you have a few large "no's" marked, leave and go to the next home. If there are only small objections that you feel you can overcome, still go to the next home because it might offer fewer negatives and a few more positives. You're not going to get **everything;** people who **build** don't even get that most of the time. Maybe you can settle for "almost exactly" what you want.

Let's assume you have found a house you feel you'll buy. **Now** is the time to get a bit picky and look at the light fixtures, the brand of kitchen appliances, door knobs, and maybe how you think it will look with your wallpaper and paint. Enjoy this time because you're almost in your new home.

FINAL DECISION

In narrowing your choice down to two or three houses, count up the" yea's" and "nay's" of each one to make that final decision. Then you'll have to determine if the home with the most "yea's" is more to your liking than the one with a few less. Hey, nobody said it was easy.

That checklist is important because you simply love this one house that is a bit more than you wanted to pay. Now, do you think you can get the seller down on the price? How much are you willing to pay? Can you possibly afford it? Perhaps the last house is better for you?

Go look through it again and keep that checklist (or my book) with you. If you definitely decide you like this one, it's time to present an offer to the Realtor and wait for a decision. You've done all you need to do . . . **for now!**

While you're waiting for a reply from your Realtor, let's go over what you've done and a list of the most **common mistakes** most new homebuyers make. Take this time to see if there is anything you overlooked.

1.   Don't waste time walking into **every** home the realtor lists:

The computer will eliminate many. The "comp" sheet will eliminate more. And the **drive-by** should eliminate more than that. Eliminate quickly what you **know** you won't like.

2.   Don't fall in love with a particular room:

Many people—men people and women people alike—see a large den with cathedral ceiling, skylight, fireplace, large picture window looking out at a giant oak tree and this seems to mesmerize them to where they hardly see much else.

Deal with this **academically** and use that checklist because you will not spend all of your time in that den, or extra-large walk-in closet, or that spacious kitchen or beautiful bathroom. Of course, if a house you can afford has **all** of these amenities and you decide you don't want it, call me and **I'll buy it!**

3.   Don't become enamored with the way the home is **furnished,** because:

Your furniture will **not** look the same! This is sort of a "trick" warning because, in the part of this book that tells about **selling** a house, we tell the seller to do **precisely** this.

You've all seen these model homes set up that look absolutely gorgeous, but please know that **your** home will not look **exactly** the same unless you buy this **exact** furniture.

> If the people who are trying to sell their home to you have either extremely good taste or they read my book, they'll use this. See the advantage you have by buying my book? If **they** read it and you **didn't,** you would have been captivated by the furnishings and make an unsound judgment.

Try to picture the home empty. In your minds-eye, place **your** furnishing in there where their beautiful furnishings are because when you buy the house, the present owners **and** their lifestyle as well as their exquisite furnishings will be gone! All you'll have is empty rooms and **your** furniture needs to fit.

4.   Persevere!

Here's one I hear all the time. "Tom, I'm so tired of looking at homes that the next one I see that looks sorta' okay, I'm going to buy it." I say **don't, stop, nope, halt, uh-uh, no-no** and any other four-letter word that is not obscene.

Don't let this happen to you! If you're tired of looking and/or can't make up your mind(s) and there isn't any time left on the sale of your present home for the new owners to move in, I say go out and **rent** for a month or so or as long as it takes to find what you want.

This isn't a **pizza** you're buying or even a new car; it's the largest investment you'll probably make in your entire life! Take your time! I know it's not a small expense to move and to store some of your furnishings but far **better** than getting a home that you'll have to remodel, repair and rebuild.

5.   Not listening to your inspector:

This is a major problem. You hired the guy to tell you what was right or wrong about the house but you've been looking for months, you're tired, you and your spouse are starting to get on each others nerves.

You want this house to be sound, you're ready to move in, yet the inspector gives you a list of repairs that should be done. Be patient! Have whatever needs to be done **before** you buy it. But you're in a hurry and you don't want to hear this; you want **good** news.

Believe it, this is good news! The inspector found patches in the roof that will, soon, leak. Cost? About $8,000 to remedy. The slab has shifted and is ready to crack. Cost? It'll bring tears to your eyes. The rafters in the attic are starting to sag. Cost? A trip to the loan company if you have pay for it.

Please, I implore you, heed my advice. I say, **walk away!** Walk away and start looking at other houses. When you find something major wrong, make the seller fix it or pass it up and continue searching.

Whatever **is** wrong, mark it down on that large pad I asked you to carry at your side. If the offer you gave your Realtor is refused and the seller wants less than the asking price but more than you're willing to pay, use this list of repairs to begin . . .

Chapter 5

NEGOTIATING THE DEAL

This is going to be a relatively short chapter because there are only a few options. The seller wants a certain price and you either can't afford it or don't want to pay that much. How do you negotiate?

USE YOUR REALTOR

The easiest way is to get your **Realtor** involved. They represent you and whatever you offer, the Realtor is obligated to take that offer to the seller. The seller now has the option to (a) accept your offer (b) reject your offer or (c) make a counter offer—perhaps concessions. Let's say the seller decides to . . .

ACCEPT YOUR OFFER

You make and offer once you've checked out the entire home, have that list of repairs with you and send that along with the offer. You submitted what you feel is a fair price and you make this offer through your Realtor and wait for an answer. If the offer is accepted, you are on your way to owning a house. Or, perhaps the seller decides to . . .

REJECT YOUR OFFER

In my experience and research, only **frightfully low** offers are downright rejected. There's nothing more to say on this except if the offer is rejected, you can always come back with a counter offer that is more reasonable, one that you can afford, and more in the "ballpark" of the asking price. Then, the seller might . . .

MAKE A COUNTER OFFER

This is when your offer is not too far off the price the seller is asking. Now, the ball is in your court. You can either accept it, reject it or come back with yet another offer, higher than the last but not as much as the seller originally asked. This is negotiating.

CONCESSIONS

There are two points of view, depending if we're **buying** or **selling.** If you own a house that you're trying to **sell** you say, "The roof will need to be replaced in about two years. A new one will cost about $5,000. I'll cut $5,000 off the price and let's make the deal." This is a form of concession and/or counter offer.

If you are the one **buying** the house, you feel the roof needs repair now, not **two years from now,** and it will cost about **$8000!** You send back the Realtor with this new offer saying you'll settle for **$7000** off the price and make the deal.

Other types of concessions might be if the **owner** is willing to pay all closing costs (or much of them). Another might be in the form or furniture, fixtures or appliances.

Perhaps there's a large chandelier that the owner

planned to take with them looks *sooo* good that you'd like it to stay and the owner might sell it to you at a very reasonable price or throw it in to make the sale.

A seller is asking $125,00 for his house but the buyer wants certain things added in. They want the drapes to stay, they want the bird bath in the back yard and they'd like to have the lawn mower, edger and garden tools.

As the **seller**, you're moving **to** an apartment and the buyer is moving **from** an apartment. Why not leave the tools? If you try to sell them you get maybe 15 or 20 cents on the dollar or less. Compromise! Make some concessions. Don't lose the sale!

SMART NEGOTIATING

Most of the time, you're in more of a command position than the seller . . . **if** you are willing to walk away from the house. A seller wants to sell, and is getting a lot of money on the sale of this house. Let's say the selling price is $150,000. An anxious seller might take $135,000. Try for this lower price and then negotiate.

To negotiate with a seller—with anyone—you should be aware of the **cost** of things. If you find several "problem areas" in the house you are going to make a bid on, find out what they will cost to repair or replace. This way, you can negotiate with a degree of intelligence. Yes, arm yourself with knowledge and this book is a good start.

ARE THERE ANY TRICKS IN MAKING AN OFFER

I wouldn't call them **tricks,** just more smart negotiating. I'd walk through that house with a large pad and pencil marking down **everything** that needs repairing or replacing. I'd list the chipped paint, the piece of rotted wood near the roof, the fact that they had a treatment for termites 6 months ago (means they might still be there) and if there is a crack in the driveway.

I'd list the light socket that has no cover plate, the fact that the insulation in the attic is maybe 6 inches here, 4 inches there and bare ceiling showing someplace else.

I would note that the fence is 8 years old with the bottom of each board rotting, the air conditioner compressor is 14 years old and doesn't seem to be adequately cooling the house on the hotter days, and that the cover on the spa is *sun-worn* and shredded.

If you've done your homework by checking out prices of these repairs, I'd put down the costs next to the gripes. Then, give this list to the Realtor along with your earnest money contract and your offer. The seller then has those three options again. To . . . accept the deal, reject it, make a counter offer.

As far as repairs that need to be made, do take the time and price them! If the seller doesn't make them (or lower the price for you) they will add up! **Take the time now!** After you buy is too late!

I emphasize **taking time** when looking because by taking time, you can make a thorough inspection. And by taking time to negotiate, it might be more money you've saved than you could earn in months. Is it worth it? **Of course it is!**

REAL ESTATE ATTORNEY

Some homebuyers use a Realtor (agent, broker) to find the house then negotiate through a real estate attorney. The difference between a real estate attorney and a regular attorney is the same as the difference between a Podiatrist and a Gynecologist; each works in different areas of their respective businesses.

A law degree used to automatically license an attorney to sell real estate. But that has changed. An attorney who specializes in real estate must also pass the licensing requirements to become an agent.

They are versed in real estate law and they should be master negotiators. If you find one who is willing to work for you, they can negotiate, draw up the legal papers and make certain you are protected under the law.

Of course, a Realtor can start the proceedings and the title company and loan officer for the title company do the rest. They do, however, get an attorney involved anyway. I'm not saying which to choose, only that you have the option.

If you aren't aware of the various things to look for in purchasing a home, I'd strongly recommend that you hire an **inspector**. If you want to be as certain as possible that this home is in the condition you'd like it to be, it's worth hiring someone knowledgeable to go over it for you **before** you make an offer or present an earnest money contract. In the words of Mr. Goodwrench, "Pay me now or—**pay** me later!"

Chapter 6

GETTING A GOOD INSPECTION

TYPES OF INSPECTIONS

Banks want inspections because they realize many homeowners don't know that much about homes, except how to **live** in them. They want to protect themselves and their mortgage. The first is the . . .

HOME INSPECTION

This is an overall inspection done by a licensed home inspector to check out the structure; the roof, the plumbing for leaks and to make certain the water runs, the appliances work, that the wiring is sound and that the foundation isn't cracked.

If this inspector is good, he not only protects the mortgage company, he also protects you! If you learn of these problems now, they can be handled before you buy the house. If they aren't, chances are you won't get a mortgage until they are solved.

It also lets you get out of your earnest money contract if you find too many things wrong with the house that weren't discovered by your own walk-thru inspection.

I recommend you meet this inspector when he arrives and walk around with him as he inspects. Ask as many questions as you like, especially about things that will help you when you have to perform maintenance or repairs, if you decide to buy this house.

TERMITE INSPECTION

This inspection is (or should be) done on each house. In fact, it's one of the few inspections it seems **all** homeowners are aware of . . . and should be. I know most of you either saw or heard of Arnold Schwarzenegger as the Terminator. Well, the termites, if left unattended, can cause more destruction than Arnie.

If termites are discovered, don't panic! They can be treated and controlled. Once a home has been treated for termites, all you need is maybe a **yearly** inspection to keep them away. Your pest control man who treats your home for roaches or your yard for fleas or fire ants will inspect and treat for termites.

My first book, **Home Improvement,** (Homeowners Most Often Asked Questions) goes into detail on how to do your **own** termite inspection.

People are scared to death of termites. Just make certain you have this inspection done **before** you purchase a house and have it done by a **licensed** or **certified** inspector. Call a professional.

MECHANICAL INSPECTION

This is optional, and not often required by most mortgage companies on **new** homes. It **is** required, however, on older homes, **especially** if a home has been vacant for several months because that's when they break—when they aren't used. It's well worth the extra cost. It's in the $100 price range.

This Mechanical Inspection is done by the HVAC man, the air conditioning and heating and ventilating inspector. This tells you whether your air conditioning system is in good working order, the age of it, the condition, the output of air as compared to the square footage of your home and the distribution of air into various rooms.

Those of you who listen to my program will often hear a caller having trouble in getting air into this room, or too much air flows into that room. This inspector can pinpoint these problems and tell you how to remedy them.

In the cold part of the world where the heating systems are intricate and paramount, they check for a cracked heat exchanger or faulty wiring and the efficiency of the heater, same as they do with the air conditioner in the warmer parts of the world.

The Structural Inspection and Termite Inspection are required. However, for safety, comfort and expense, I'd strongly suggest you get a **Mechanical Inspection** as well, even if they aren't required. It's smart buying.

If a home hasn't been occupied for a while, get this HVAC Inspection. Air conditioning systems often break down more when not being used because the seals tend to dry up and crack. The **working parts** get constant oiling when the unit is in use.

When a home hasn't been occupied for several months (or longer) there is usually trouble with the water system too. The water heater is reasonably inexpensive to replace but the pipes could have been frozen and burst or rusted out, the faucets rusted, any number of things could go wrong.

Remember, these inspections protect you, more than the mortgage company. If a home is passed and something breaks or collapses after you buy the house, it's you, not the mortgage company, seller or the inspector, who is responsible for these repairs or replacements.

That's why the inspections are so very important. They don't **guarantee** that things will stay perfect, but they are wise moves to make because a few hundred against several thousand dollars (for unknown repairs) is a worthwhile trade.

HOW TO FIND THESE INSPECTORS

Realtors are not supposed to give you the name of an inspector. They can, however, furnish you with a **list** of inspectors from which you might choose. (Another rule set down because somebody cheated.) If you can't get such a list from your real estate agent, find a person who recently bought a home and ask them about their inspector(s).

HOW TO CHOOSE THE RIGHT ONE

In many states, in order to become a licensed inspector, you merely have to take a few classes and pass a test. Many go to school, take the test, pass it, and still know little about what they're doing. They do it for side money. I'd choose a guy with a structural engineering degree or maybe a former home builder.

When calling an inspector, ask for their background and references. If they say they are a licensed engineer, that they are working for a company that does foundation design, that should be good enough. If they are a retired home builder who is just staying active, that's okay too.

There's no reason to be wary of every person who says they are an inspector. But, be smart. Ask for credentials and if they hesitate or can't provide proof, pass them by. If they do seem competent, still check with a client or two before you make up your mind.

Go to their office and see if it's run in a businesslike way. I'd ask for a look at some of their recent reports that they made on other houses. Look and see if these reports seem adequate and how complete they are. Take this extra time to be certain. You'll be glad you did!

INSPECTORS RESPONSIBILITY

They are responsible for the condition of the home at the **time** they make their inspection. If he turns on the hot water and it's hot, if he turns on the oven and it heats, if he flicks a switch and the lights are working, the air conditioner is cooling, the heater is heating and the foundation isn't cracked, his responsibility as far as that inspection is complete.

Perhaps the slab was cracked—and repaired—and the inspector says it looks okay to him. Then, in a year or two something happens, something moves, and the slab is cracked again. That inspector is not responsible.

I'd find an inspector who is tough, rigid in his appraisal, and proud of his work. These types are your true friends although you've never met them before and probably won't ever see them again.

The inspector has the final word on a home. Once they write that report and send it to the mortgage company, that's it. Either what is faulty is repaired and a new inspection is made that passes, or the mortgage company is not interested. **Appreciate** that report because it's to your best interest.

> When you decide on an inspector, ask them if you can walk around with them. The "norm" for a complete inspection is about 4 hours and the inspector would like to have 3 of those hours on their own. That last hour is yours to ask questions. Don't be afraid to ask anything you don't understand or feel you need to know.

There have been cases when one inspector puts "thumb down" on an inspection, for instance, that the roof was bad and the mortgage company refuses to loan on that home until the roof is **repaired.** It must be done either by the present owner (seller) or some concession made by the seller to the buyer who then, must fix that roof. Let's say the deal is off.

Then the next day a **new** buyer looks at the house and their inspector says the roof is okay and the loan is with another mortgage company. The deal goes through and in a year or two, the roof caves in. It's a cruel world out there. Do you see why a rigid inspection is important?

When I go out to inspect for a potential home buyer, many agents who know me **shudder** because I am tough on these inspections. I know all that can go wrong and I know the signs of something that is "about" to go wrong and I list this on the comment part of the report.

The smart real estate agents appreciate this because their reputation is as important as their time. To throw out a worn cliche, "It really is a small world" and an agent's reputation can result in a highly successful career or, it can be a short-lived one.

FINAL REPORT

A Realtor friend of mine called me just a few days ago to look at an inspection report that was given to one of her clients. The inspector wrote up about 8 pages of "stuff" that was absurd, but it scared the dickens out of the potential buyer, who was ready to walk away.

The home, only three years old, was in perfect shape. But, the inspector, either wanting to make an impression on the Realtor or mortgage company, made a list of repairs that amounted to $1300.

They listed a few outside bricks that needed to be caulked, that paint was peeling from a small area on the garage, that the valve behind the washing machine needed to be replaced and more *stupid stuff* that should have not been mentioned.

> Whenever you buy a home—even a new one—there will be these "little" things that need to be tended too. Count on spending a few hundred dollars on these insignificant items that will eventually happen anyway.

Yet another item he marked was that the wood part of the house had recently been covered by aluminum siding and he wasn't sure about the shape of the wood behind it. That, to me, is a giant **red flag**, because most of you know of my feelings about siding and the fact that far too often it's put up to "hide" rotting wood.

I asked that they take a closer look at what was "behind" the siding. I found out, just a few hours ago, that the wood behind it was in good shape and that the house was sold. See, I have no vendetta against siding; I just call it the way I see it!

Just remember, **use** these inspectors! Walk through the attic with them. They will point out, *See there. That little knee brace needs replacing. It's not a big deal but really* *should be taken care of,* and things like that. You learn a lot by walking with and talking to the inspectors.

Some of what he might tell you isn't even marked in his report because it's slight, but it's good to know. And, if you walk around with him, you'll know in 15 minutes or so whether the guy is competent or an idiot.

On this **Final Report** that is sent to you, sit down and read through it carefully, either with the inspector or with a friend who is in the building or remodeling business, and go over each point.

STORY

This isn't my "barbecue the inspectors" section but I have to tell you about this one because I was recently involved in it.

Another Realtor friend called me to come take a look at an inspection list made on a house they were trying to sell. The buyer was concerned about a cracked slab and wanted my opinion on it.

The inspector had marked on his report that, five years ago, the foundation on this particular house had been repaired and as far as he was concerned, the foundation had not moved. That was a common-sense call. If the slab hadn't moved in 5 years, chances were high that the repair job did the trick.

As I read further in the report, the inspector

recommend **gutters** for the house. He stated that the house "used to have gutters" and these gutters would **prevent** water from puddling next to the foundation causing it to move.

The buyer didn't know what kind of gutters to get (galvanized, plastic or rain handlers) and wanted my opinion as to whether he should get them at all.

When I looked further in the report for the **date** the slab was repaired (same date the gutters were removed and **never put back)** I realized that the house needed to not have gutters! In this particular climate, the rain coming down the roof was sufficient to keep the ground around the foundation **moist**.

I noticed that the flower beds around the house were healthy. This very well could have been the result of the **water coming off the roof** as well a regular watering by the occupant. The "gutter" statement tipped me off and gutters should not have been recommended.

By just looking at the report a bit closer, I was able to save the home buyer about $2000 on gutters, but more importantly, make them feel comfortable about the slab, and to **prevent** the repaired slab from cracking again.

What happened is that the inspector told the lady to water her garden and to make certain she watered around the house to keep the foundation moist. Then, in the same breath, he tells her to put in gutters; contradictory statements.

Somehow or other, Mother Nature was doing the job expertly and in the words of some wise person, "If it ain't broke, don't fix it."

Last tip on this inspector stuff is to make certain you find a competent inspector and that the report is detailed and neat so you can read it. Then, do read it and look for clues or get it to that friend who is or was a builder.

Part II

Chapter 7

WHAT IS YOUR HOME WORTH

The object is to find a **realistic** selling price. Let your Realtor help; they know what other homes in the neighborhood and in your area are selling for.

You can also drive around looking at *For Sale By Owner* signs and disturb the ones who want to save a commission. Rarely will a person get the price they'd **like to get** for their home. Again, be realistic.

Let me begin by knocking out some of the myths many home owners have when they plan to sell.

MYTH #1

My home has appreciated in value. The price of land has gone up dramatically in my area, the cost of lumber and other fixtures and appliance has gone up, so I should be able to sell at a higher price.

Maybe . . . but probably not! It all depends on how old your home is, how well you've maintained it, and the current buying/selling market.

The real estate market tends to run in cycles. If you bought at the **top** of a cycle, perhaps your home has **depreciated** vastly. If you bought at the **bottom** of the cycle, your home probably **appreciated** considerably.

MYTH #2

I put in a hot tub, swimming pool and an apartment on top of my garage. I remodeled my bathroom with a large tub. I put in hardwood floors, a new roof, and had my home professionally landscaped. I know it's worth more.

It has increased in value. But the hot tub, swimming pool, bathroom, floors, roof and landscaping are not especially **assets** to increase value. I explain many of those in detail later on in the book. The only increase in value I can see is the garage apartment because it increases the **square footage.**

Realtors are **allowed**—but not **advised**—to quote square footage because there's too much margin for error through measurement and interpretation. Some homeowners want to include a garage as square footage and if it's attached to the house, it can be. Others want to include a carport as square footage and it isn't. See? Interpretation can get you into trouble.

The items you mentioned will enhance the looks and **salability** of your home and maybe a slight bit more than the other homes for sale in your neighborhood. But, if other homes are run down and raggedy, if the neighborhood has not kept up their landscaping, your home will stick out like a sore thumb and few want a high-priced home in a low-priced neighborhood. Let me give you an example of what I mean.

STORY

I have a friend who bought into an apartment building that was converted to condominiums. This happened maybe 25 years ago when apartment conversions were the thing to do. He paid $25,000 for this "apartment" and proceeded to put in extras.

He put extra walls in to shut out the normal noises from adjoining apartments. He cut a part from his large master bedroom and ran a neat, mirrored closet with sliding doors across the width of the room thereby giving him an added 24 feet of hanger space.

He had an expensive rock fountain and waterfall put on his small patio. He ripped out the wall between his bedroom and bath and put in an Italian Marble oversized tub with jacuzzi. He went so far as installing a "no noise" toilet, bidet, a shelf over the tub for his TV and a small refrigerator that held iced tea and champagne.

He even went so far as to (ingeniously) put some pieces together from a washing machine and run a copper pipe over his window that was punctured with holes. With a control panel next to his bed, he could touch one switch and the drapes over the huge picture window eased open. And when he touched yet another switch, it **rained** over his window! Needless to point out, he was a bachelor.

He had the conventional stairs knocked out and put new ones in that spiraled and he installed a floor safe. He also remodeled his kitchen and entry (again using expensive Italian Marble) and when it was all over, he had over **$80,000** invested. Did he have a chance of recovering any of these extravagant amenities? **Not likely!**

He sold this dream pad, located in a complex that was not highly maintained and where the average condo was now selling for as little as $20,000, and at the **bottom cycle** in the real estate market. He was willing to take a "hickey" and put it up for sale for $60,000, twenty thousand less than what he had in it. He had over-built (or over accessorized) dramatically.

He moved to another condominium on the water and his bachelor "trap" stayed on the market for almost two years. In the meantime, there were several other units for sale in the complex, many that sold on foreclosure. The market had risen slightly but he could never get anywhere near his price. He finally sold for the $25,000 he originally paid for the place.

MYTH #3

I'll put a high sales price on my home, then come down and make the people think they're getting a deal.

Your idea is **multi-flawed**; here's why. First, you run the chance of "missing" some serious, qualified buyers because they will shop the neighborhood and buy another house.

Second, if you **lower** the price and are working though a Realtor, they will have those **former prices** listed and it just causes buyers to think about why you're lowering it. *Has something broken that we can't detect? Is the slab starting to crack? Maybe the air conditioner and heating system is too old and needs to be replaced? Maybe they **need** the money and **have** to sell?*

Third, don't fool yourself or insult the intelligence of the buyer or the buyer's agent. You're not running a couch sale at a department store putting in a low-priced item as a "loss leader", you're selling something pretty big, real property, and in an area where these buyers can look at other homes. Your home is not the only one for sale and to price it **realistically** is the answer.

MYTH #4

I don't want to listen to a broker. I know what my house is worth. I'm no dunce. I know what real estate is selling for.

I'm neither an agent nor a broker. I'm not earning a fee for saying nice things about Realtors and I'm not getting any money from the Board of Realtors. But sellers, these people have all the facts and should be consulted (and listened to) when you price your home.

If you want to sell it above what the market demands, you're just kidding yourself. Remember, a fair price for what the market will stand is the price you need to ask.

MYTH #5

I'll sell my house myself and save the commission. I can do it quicker and get to keep more money.

Wrong again! Unless you're extremely lucky. As I say over and over again throughout this book, Realtors have the advantage of that Multiple Listing Service and every Realtor who has that service is a potential salesperson for your home. Instead of just one person—you—trying to sell it, you have **thousands**.

I've discovered that most of the time a buyer who is shopping and sees that *For Sale By Owner* sign in your front yard will automatically **deduct** what they feel the commission would be in their heads and offer you less.

They know you're trying to save money and, more often than not, it ends up the same price (or less) than a Realtor could have gotten for you. Don't be "Penny wise and pound foolish."

You'll have people knocking on your house during any time of day (or night) instead of having the **Realtor** schedule them at your convenience. You'll also have to keep your house clean and tidy **at all times!** You'll be getting calls (day and night) with people asking you a multitude of questions, many that are absurd. I say the price of a Realtor is cheap. Be smart. Earn money the way you know how and pay those who know how to sell your home for their service.

MYTH #6

I need an attorney to watch out for my interest.

Why? The title company has an attorney to verify that the contract is legal. You pay for a **Title Policy**, and this policy is insurance that protects you and the mortgage company. Chances are you won't even see this attorney, only his fee on the closing papers.

I think an **excellent** chapter for both buyer and seller to read is Chapter 5, Part I (page 72, I think) titled **Negotiating The Deal.** I had to put it someplace but it deals mainly with **compromise.** It gives the buyer and seller each others' viewpoints and helps consummate the sale.

Chapter 8

SELL BY OWNER OR AGENCY

Realtors often work a better deal for the buyer and/or the seller depending which they represent. Realtors are taught to follow a procedure that is smart, legal, and ethical. It's the same as in a lawsuit; *It's best not to represent yourself.*

WHAT A REALTOR DOES

In Part I of this book, I advised the **buyer** to use a Realtor and now, it's time to tell you how a Realtor can help you, the **seller.**

Let's begin with the **listing** Realtor, the one who gets the information from the present homeowner. A good Realtor won't just take any price on a listing; they work with and educate the seller in order to get a **realistic** price. (There's that word again.)

Naturally, owners want the highest price they can get and many have unreal expectations. It's up to the **Realtor** to show the owner comparables in that neighborhood. Realtors often advise owners on what they can reasonably expect to get for their property and together, they try to work out a fair market value. After all, each wants the home to sell.

The Realtor, using a **Listing Form,** will then measure the outside of the home—including the garage—and each room and closet inside the home. They will list items such as an air conditioner, heater, fireplace, oven, range, dishwasher, disposal, whether it has a fire smoke and/or burglar alarm and any item the owner feels will be left with the house such as refrigerator, deep freeze, microwave oven, washer, dryer, 2000 pound floor safe and their 12-year old toothless cocker spaniel.

This listing form has the asking price, address, subdivision, city, date the owner will vacate, lot size, style of the home, whether it's a one or two story, if there's a sidewalk, paved street, size of patio, type of fence, if it has a heated pool, and the length and depth of that pool.

They list school districts, whether the nearby schools are public, private or parochial, elementary, junior high, high school or college. They also list financial information such as amount of first or second lien, interest rate, the name of the listing agent, and that agent's night and day phone number.

They also list the showing instructions like *vacant* and when the owner (if not vacant) wants it to be shown. It tells if there is a lock box, an alarm, instructions for the alarm and for showing. On one page you can see it all—**almost!**

The Texas Association of Realtors has what is called a *Seller's Disclosure Notice* which the listing agent helps the owner fill out. This list asks even more questions and the seller(s) is asked to check off **each item** that will remain in the home.

The seller is to sign that they are (or are not) aware

that each of these items is in working condition, that the house has (or does not have) any defects or is in need of repair.

Other items include: Range, dishwasher, microwave, washer/dryer hookups, security system, tv antenna, ceiling fan(s), central AC, window units, plumbing system, patio/decking, pool, pool equipment, fireplace & chimney, wood burning or gas, gas lines, oven, trash compactor, window screens, fire detection equipment, cable TV wiring, attic fan(s), outdoor grill, sauna, pool heater, disposal, rain gutters, intercom system, satellite dish, exhaust fan(s), public sewer system, fences, spa, lawn sprinkler system, gas fixtures, light switches, garage, garage door opener, water heater, water supply, insulation, roof, and on and on.

Still another part of this lists talks about the condition of the interior and exterior walls, roof, fences, plumbing, sewers, septic tank, ceilings, doors, foundation/slab, driveways, electrical system, floors, windows, basement, sidewalks, and lighting fixtures.

There are still more questions, such as termite or wood damage needing repair, **previous** termite damage, treatment, **previous** flooding, improper drainage, water penetration, located in 100-year floodplain, present flood insurance coverage, landfill, fault lines, underground storage tanks, wetlands on property, previous structural or roof repairs, hazardous or toxic waste, asbestos components in your insulation, ureformaldehyde insulation (formaldehyde with urethane coating), radon gas, lead base paint, aluminum wiring, **previous** fires, unplatted easements, subsurface structure or pits, and more that I can't think of at the moment.

In the event this list doesn't cover everything under the sun, they ask the owner, **point blank,** if there is **anything**—any item or equipment **not** mentioned in the list—that is in need of repair.

Then, on each of these items, the owner warrants that they are there (if they're there), whether they are working and if not, they must **explain** why not and whether they intend to fix them or not.

The next paragraph asks whether the owner is aware of room additions, structural modifications, alterations or repairs made without necessary permits or not in compliance with the local building codes.

If the seller knowingly **lies,** and the buyer finds out, they can cancel the contract and sue for **treble damages** including punitive damages for grief, pain, anguish and attorney's fees. It is a **state law** you are breaking and once you sign that contract falsely, all the marbles are in the plaintiff's court.

Buyers reading this will ask, *Why then, should I hire an inspector?* Because, sellers might not **be aware** of all that is wrong. Inspectors will find out!

When this form is signed, the Realtor will put a *For Sale* sign in the yard. This sign lists the number of the **Realtor,** not the owner. This way, the owner isn't disturbed by all sorts who knock on their door asking the standard question, *How much are you selling your house for?*

The **listing** Realtor then takes a photograph (or two or three) of the house they just listed and goes to their office to begin more work. They list the home with their MLS computer bank that goes to every Realtor in the city.

> The Realtor who **took the listing** for the house doesn't automatically become the same person who **sells** the house! A selling agent can be **any** licensed real estate person.

HOW MUCH THE REALTOR MAKES

Ah yes! Everybody is concerned over how much it will cost them for this service. I'll tell you what I thought, probably what you thought, and what it really is!

I thought it was a standard fee of 6% of the selling price, didn't you? But one of the foremost Realtors in the city told me differently. They said there is **no set fee** or *standard fee*. That a Realtor who lists the house works with the seller and they, **together,** determine the fee.

I spoke to Al Davis, a Realtor in Austin, about my thinking 6% was standard and he said that it wasn't, but that any less and the Realtor can't survive. He gave me this example.

Let's say (for the sake of argument) that the fee **is 6% of the selling price** of a particular home. The **listing** agent, when the home sells, is entitled to **3%** (or half) of this commission. The **selling** agent gets the other half.

And then, it depends whether or not the selling agent is working for a broker, and what these arrangements are. If the selling agent is working for a broker, the percentage of this **half** commission is cut even more. Usually, **1%** goes to the broker.

So you see, sellers and home buyers, these real estate people work hard for their money and the percentage is cut and cut again. It costs money for an office, telephone, organization dues, a nice 4-door automobile (whether they like 4 doors or not, they need it for taking buyers and their families around). They have gasoline expense, car repair, equipment to buy and rent, advertising etc. It cost money to be in business.

I know. I **know!** You work hard for your money too. But, but we're not talking about you! What I want to do is neither seek pity for, nor **canonize** these real estate people. I just want you to be aware that they're not all getting rich and probably **none will retire** from the measly commission they make from listing or selling your home.

THE SELLING AGENT

A sale is negotiated through the selling agent by a prospective home buyer. Let's say the home lists for $150,000 and all the buyer can pay (or wants to pay) is $135,000. They make an offer on an Earnest Money contract for that amount and the agent (or Realtor) takes it to the listing agent who then takes it to the seller.

The seller says all they are willing to come down, for a quick sale with the home in an "as is" condition, is to 140,000. The listing agent takes the offer back to the selling agent to take back to the buyer. (This takes a lot of time!)

The buyer says maybe they can get the extra money for the $5000 but they want this and that fixed. The selling agent calls the listing agent who, in turn, calls the seller. They talk. It could go back and fourth five or six times before anything is settled.

There are **thousands** of different case-scenarios carried on each day like this. The owner says his house is worth more because it has a swimming pool and the buyer has three kids and doesn't even want a pool. Therefore, the extra money the seller asking because of the pool is a **negative** to the buyer.

The **Realtor** is in the middle of all of this. Sometimes, the buyer and/or the seller becomes irate and the agent is in the middle of this too! They must "keep their cool" at all times in acting as a "go-between" for these two people.

Chapter 9

HOW TO PREPARE YOUR HOME TO SELL

CREATING CURB APPEAL

Remember in Chapter 6 when I talked to **buyers** about driving by a home to see if it looks good? That if it does look good you stop, and if it doesn't, then you keep on driving? Well in **selling** a home, if they don't stop you don't have a chance at all. So "curb appeal" is what you are shooting for—initially.

The bottom line is, if it looks good in front, if the door is not hanging on to the hinges, if the yard is cut, hedges trimmed, the grass is edged and the driveway is not cracked or cluttered with *things*, the chances of a person stopping is increased tenfold. Here are some suggestions to follow to make *lookers* come inside for a walk-thru and, possibly, become **buyers**!

> To make it easier on you, use this book as a **checklist**. Get a **red pencil**, and no need to write anything down; just **circle** what you've done in this book, then buy another book from the additional money you've made by selling your home quickly and at a good price.

Remember? Put a red circle over the *a, b, c,* or the *1, 2, 3* etc. When it's all circled, you're ready. If you don't do these things, people drive on by. Be smart about it. Get your ten bucks worth out of this book.

MY RECOMMENDATIONS

1.   **Keep** your yard freshly mowed and **edged.** It makes your yard appear well kept, and grass growing over the concrete walkway or drive looks awful.

2.   Weed the flower beds, trim the hedges and trees. **KTRH** has a *Yard of the Month* contest where they give over a **thousand dollars** of prizes to the person who has the most attractive front yard. You'd be surprised how nice your yard will look if you cut a few limbs and trim a few hedges and shape a few plants.

There are flowers and shrubs that you can buy for a few dollars each, and it's unbelievable how a few here and a few there spruce up an otherwise dull-looking front yard.

Buy a couple of plants in pots to put on your sparse, cold, concrete porch (more things you can take with you when you move) and maybe a few hanging baskets.

3.   Keep the driveway and walkway swept. If you're the type that has an old junker that you work on, please, give it away, bury it in a deep hole or hide it at some other house!

If you have such a vehicle you've worked on, do whatever you can to get that oil and grease off your driveway and/or garage floor. Use the formula for grease removal or paint the driveway, but get those horrid, unattractive stains **off!**

TO REMOVE STAINS FROM CONCRETE

Pour Mineral Spirits over the stained area. Then take some clay **cat litter** and scatter that over the stain and the mineral spirits. Then, get a **brick** and grind the cat litter into the mineral spirits. Let it set overnight, then sweep it up. If it's a stubborn stain, do it a second time, or a third, but try. If the stains are old, you'll probably never get them all up.

4.   If your home has mildew on the outside walls, a simple solution of bleach mixed with equal parts water in a sprayer will take it all off. If you don't have a sprayer and can't borrow one, put the bleach on with a mop or rags while the sun is shining. A few hours later, hose it off with water.

If your hands will come into contact with this solution, wear rubber gloves because the bleach, even with a half water mixture, can play havoc with skin.

5.   Ask your neighbor's help. Hopefully you have neat neighbors. If not, and you're friends, ask them to clean up their act for a few days. If they won't trim their hedges, you trim them! If they're too lazy to cut their grass, ask them if you can cut it! I promise you, it's worth the effort because (again) what I tell home buyers to be **aware of**, I'm telling you, to remedy.

6.   Give the front of your home an inspection as if you were a West Point upperclassman inspecting a platoon of plebes. Walk up to your front door if there's dirt on it, wash it off. If the door is scratched, repaint it. If there

are cobwebs in the corners, sweep them off. And, buy a new mat. When you sell the home, take the mat with you.

It's just *common sense* to know that if the outside of your home is not perfect, and the people come up to ring the bell to gain entry, they have a few moments to stand there, looking at all sorts of things; the doorknob, any visible separation between the doors, whether the doorbell is broken, at the mud daubers nest above their head, spider webs, and all kinds of things that seem inconsequential but "turn off" a prospective buyer.

7.   The front windows too. They should be washed or wiped. Take the screens off and get the dead bugs from the window sill, you know, the space **between** the screens and the actual window. There's nothing less appealing that a *lizard skeleton* staring at you.

8.   Whatever needs nailing, screwing, cleaning or painting, **do it now!** Not any of this will increase the value of your home but everything I mentioned won't cost over a hundred bucks and doesn't take a lot of time. Anybody but the extremely lazy can do it.

SETTING THE STAGE INSIDE THE HOUSE

1.   Other than vacuuming, sweeping, mopping and polishing, get some cutesy little items like bowls with fresh fruit, freshly cut flowers, maybe even some lace doilies you had never used since they were given to you 20 years ago as a wedding present. Make the house look cozy and comfortable.

2.   Place house slippers on the throw rug right near your bed; get these people in the "feel" of this place being their home. In your bathroom, how about a bowl of scented potpourri, and **clean** face towels.

3.   If it's winter or cold, light up that fireplace and put some hot cocoa on the stove to give the house a friendly, lived-in smell. Leave a bottle of wine in view with maybe a few glasses and hope these lookers aren't staunch non-drinkers.

> Take the chance; the majority of people (according to some surveys) enjoy wine and if not, it will offend but a few. They don't have to **drink** the wine, just see it there.

4.   If you have animals that live in the house that are not potty-trained, clean it up. If these animals live mostly inside, they might have an odor. Oh, none you'll recognize; you've become **immune** to the smell but non-animal people will detect it in a microsecond. It's the same if you are a . . .

5.   Smoker. As rabid as many are about smoking, that smoke smell can be detected faster than skunk perfume; so **spray!** Open your windows for as long as it doesn't rain in and try to get rid of that smoke odor.

I have a *No Smoking* rule in my house. A friend of mine who visited for a few days observed that rule . . . in our **presence**. But, when he "went to the bathroom" to sit and read the morning paper, he sneaked a cigarette, reasoning the exhaust fan would blow away the smoke and the smell. It didn't!

The smell seeped under and around the doors and came into the main part of the house. It took a week to get that one-cigarette smell out.

To rid your home of **cigarette smoke,** wipe the walls with white vinegar and water (1/2 and 1/2 mixture). Place large, shallow bowls of the same mixture on countertops and tables for three or four days or until the smell is gone. This treatment will absorb a variety of unpleasant odors including that of dead fish or live animals, plus *presents* they might leave behind.

---

6.   Maybe even have the stereo playing some "elevator music" that is not too loud, just to set the mood. And maybe a lighted candle. **Set the stage** as if you're ready for romance. In fact, that's what you have to do if you want to make a quick sale; romance the lookers.

FOCUSING ON THE POSITIVE

1.   If you have a highly energy-efficient house, further set the stage by leaving a few of the cancelled checks or maybe a recent paid electric bill in plain view. People are inquisitive and will "sneak a peek" at a check or bill for no earthly reason. Humans just do that. If they don't see them, point them out and tell them how energy-efficient the home is.

2.   If you purchased a new water heater or

refrigerator (if it stays with the house), dishwasher, trash compactor, disposal, new paint, siding, new garage door, new air conditioner compressor, recent inspections, new roof, new paint . . . point these positive items out.

3.   Talk about the improvements you've done to the home. All of these things add up. Focus on the **positive**. If you put down a new patio or tiled the bath or added cedar to a closet, keep those receipts handy. If you have warranties, instruction booklets on the appliances and air conditioner, heater, water heater, whatever, have those ready. Many of these warranties are transferable.

4.   Make your Realtor aware of these items to show to their prospect. You might not get your money back on the various items but you've certainly made it more attractive to the prospect because everybody likes a deal, everybody likes to save money, and **everybody** (hopefully) wants to hear positive things.

What you want to do is to create an atmosphere, an ambiance, a positive feeling in this house-shopper. You want them to be put at ease. Make them aware of the care you've given this home . . . maybe their new home! You want them thinking, *These people are neat. They have a comfortable home. They care about maintenance.*

5.   A nice touch is to have a typed list of the various workmen who fix the plumbing, roof, tile, electrical, the fence, those who maintain the yard, and maybe a maid or baby sitter you'd recommend. Add to that a list of the nearby ambulance service, hospital, police and emergency

pet clinic.

Make it **easy** for them and if it comes down to some other house or yours, you'll have the upper edge with this information; same as a gunfighter putting his back to the sun. You might not win but you increase the odds in your favor.

And this isn't trying to *fool* or *pull the wool* over the eyes of a potential purchaser, it's just smart business. You're not trying to trick anyone, you're just making it appealing.

WHAT NOT TO DO

Many people spend money uselessly by fixing up or replacing things in their home that will do them **no good at all!** I'll give you a list of what to do as well as a list of what not to do.

1.   Chances are I'm repeating myself, but the major thing I would do is to **clean the house!** I'd clean the walls and the carpet. If the walls have holes in them, you'll have to repair the holes and then paint. If the carpet has a stain or two, put a rug over it or a potted plant.

2.   The easiest way to brighten up a room is to paint it, but try **washing** the walls first. If you paint, the new owners might not like the color. I've found that even freshly painted homes are repainted almost immediately by a new owner. It could also have a **negative** effect on a buyer. *These people have fresh paint on their walls. I wonder what*

they're trying to hide?

3.   If the carpet **really** looks like the dickens, turn that **negative** into a **positive** by pointing out to the looker(s) the very second you approach an obvious rundown area that, *The floors look awful but I've made a very lucrative allowance that lets you put in your own floor covering.*

To take that "extra" step, give them a schematic of carpet pointing out the square yards it will take to recover whatever needs recovering along with a few bids from carpet companies and maybe even the name of a tile man or carpenter who will put in hardwood floors.

If the carpet is so horrible that you have to replace it, you're reasonably safe with a neutral color, like beige. The new owners might prefer something different, maybe even hardwood floors or tile. Don't presume that their taste is the same as yours and **don't spend money needlessly!**

(Get inexpensive carpet if it looks so ratty that you can't stand looking at it for another minute.)

STORY

A Realtor who was trying to sell a "spec" home called complaining that the yellow countertop in the kitchen caused her to lose several sales. She wanted it replaced. But the owner refused saying it would cost maybe $1500 to rip out and put in a white top.

The owner called the company who was furnishing the home display and asked for some attractive and expensive **copper cooking pots** to put on the stove as a diversion. He added a **bowl of fruit,** a few **lace dish towels** and a **bouquet of flowers** on the countertop.

He had them add a **toaster, blender** and **can opener** to put along the countertop near the sink, with more flowers on the window sill. You'd be amazed how those items took the focus from the yellow counter top.

It still took a few months before the house sold and one of the changes the buyers insisted upon was, *Get rid of that bad-taste, ostentatious, yellow countertop and replace it with a beige one or they wouldn't buy!* Take the least expensive route **first!**

4.   Clean up the garbage. We've gone over this earlier about "cleaning up your act" and this goes for taking out last nights pizza, the beer cans, underwear from the bedposts, towels from the bathroom floor, dirty laundry stacked on the washer and, **empty that cat box!**

I know you cat lovers feel your cat is neat and clean because they bury their *poop.* But *cat poop* is not one of those "Out of sight, out of mind things". You cannot bury cat poop deep enough to erase that lingering odor! Put the cat in the garage a few weeks **before** you put your house on the market, and still try my vinegar remedy.

Clean that bathtub and toilet bowl and **get a new toilet seat** for ten or so dollars. The new owners will put in their own but it is ten bucks well spent even if they toss your few-week-old one in the garbage.

Other things to do is put your *Penthouse* and *Playboy* magazines in a drawer, make your beds, wipe fingerprints from the doorknobs and around the light switches, get cleanser to work around the faucet seats by the handles in the bath and kitchen, maybe re-caulk the tile in the bathroom (inexpensive but a good touch), and alter your slovenly lifestyle while lookers walk through your house.

Clean and reorganize your storage closets and your bedroom walk-in. Throw away those leisure suits and that moth-eaten tux you haven't worn in 15 years. Get the mud from your shoes, maybe even shine them or point them toe first to the wall out of plain view.

Keep the house clean and things picked up at all times. To do this, everybody has to pitch in; kids, live-in relatives and your spouse as well as you. Once it's sold, then you can go back to living like a pig but until it is, make it and keep it neat and clean. **Set the stage!**

STORY

When I bought my house, I liked the way it looked from the outside. I had a car telephone and called the owners from the curb. They said to come on in, and the house was spotless. I had almost made up my mind already from the outside, from the back yard, the neighborhood, location to my work and schools.

Of course, I went up in the attic to check for adequate insulation, roof leaks and storage space. I checked the HVAC unit, water heater, the plumbing . . . I checked everything I tell you to check! The *coup de grace* was in finding it neat and clean.

STORY

About 8 years ago I built a home for a couple in Porter, Texas. They were living in one of the first Kingwood homes ever built and it was nothing fancy; just a roof and some walls. And this was at a time when homes weren't selling well. But this lady *set a stage* Cecile B. DeMille would have been proud of.

She was an artist, what you might call a "pottery lady" in that she had antiques and pottery, much of which was broken, cracked and/or scratched. Some of these antiques were "beat up" but she covered these breaks and spots with doilies, threw the patchwork quilt on her bed, put little throw rugs here and there, and placed flowers all over. She had a "weaving corner" with an old time Spinning Wheel. A unique setting, to be sure.

The home sold within 10 days—at full price—and during a time when you could hardly give a house away in this town. My Realtor friend called a few weeks later to tell me how the new owners were so disappointed.

They thought they were moving into this quaint farmhouse from the cover of *Collier's* magazine by *Norman Rockwell.* But, when the furniture was removed, they had only a regular home with a roof and four walls.

Yes, **set the stage!** It isn't "fooling anyone", it's showmanship. That's why I say look at everything, especially at the "little" things because, bet on the fact that the potential buyers will look at everything!

ANNOYANCES YOU SHOULD NEVER EXPERIENCE

1.   A dripping faucet.
Solution: Put a new washer in it.

2.   A dark room with the drapes closed.
Solution: Open the drapes or put in large watt light bulbs.

3.   Dirty carpet.
Solution: Rent a shampoo machine or have it professional shampooed.

4.   Peeling paint on a front door.
Solution: Repaint it.

5.   A light switch that doesn't work.
Solution: Unscrew the cover plate and see if a wire is off. Then, turn off the power and repair it.

6.   Mildew stains on tile grout.
Solution: Spray it with bleach! There are several cleaners on the market specifically for that. Ask at your local home improvement center for the latest

and the best. Try bleach first!

7.   A torn shower curtain.
Solution: Come on! It costs only a few bucks. Buy a new one!

8.   Old toilet seat.
Solution: Replace it, especially if it's one of those soft kind and some of the outer layer is ripping. As I mentioned earlier in the book, the new owner might get a new seat even if yours is new, but do it anyway.

9.   Windows that won't open.
Solution: It **could** mean that your foundation has moved and the windows are racked. Then, if they're painted, they paint could be welding them. If you have those *up* and *down* wooden windows, my grandmother ran a bar of soap along the sliding edge.

10.   A leaky toilet.
Solution: Put my vaseline remedy on the clapper and if that doesn't work get replacement parts.

11.   Scarred walls.
Solution: Patch them and touch them up.

12.   Closets jammed with clothes.
Solution: It's time to weed out those World War II things anyway.

13.   Filthy oven.
Solution: Clean it with almost any of the oven cleaners on the market. I'd try the self-cleaning type first and if that doesn't work, use "elbow grease" (scrubbing with Comet).

14.   Loose towel racks/torn towels.
Solution: Get a screwdriver and tighten the screws and put new towels up.

15.   Stained kitchen or bathroom cabinets.
Solution: If you haven't completely refinished your kitchens or painted them, at least wipe them as clean as you can, okay?

CABINET CLEANING SOLUTION

To clean and refurbish wood cabinets, here's my remedy again. Use a mixture of 2 parts mineral spirits and 1 part linseed oil and wipe the cabinets as clean as you can. If the area you just treated feels sticky, put a dab of mineral spirits on a clean cloth to wipe off the excess linseed oil.

16.   Dirty areas around light fixtures.
Solution: Try a simple solution of Soft Scrub and water or a mild abrasive and be gentle with the scrubbing, especially on wallpaper.

Many people put plastic shields around the fixtures because no matter how clean you are or how often you wash your hands, there will always be a time or two when they are soiled.

I realize much of what I'm telling you, you already know. Perhaps though, a few things you forgot and if these are done, it increases your chances of selling. Nothing is guaranteed, but let's get the odds in your favor!

You'd never attempt to try selling a car that wasn't washed, or with a flat tire or a dead battery or with a dripping radiator. It's the same with a house. **Fix** your air conditioner, heater, water faucets, etc., before you are ready to show the house. It's smart!

Chapter 10

INCREASE THE VALUE OF YOUR HOME

In preparing for this book I looked though some national home improvement books and catalogs to see if I could find anything new to tell you about. I announce happily and with complete humility, I found nothing! Some of what I did find, I disagree with and I'll tell you why.

You see, an advantage I have over these people (and that you get through my books) is that, *I do not dance to any drum beat other than my own!* I see things, I build with them, I use them in some way or other, and if they work I tell you about them. If they don't work, I tell you about them.

WHERE YOUR MONEY IS BEST SPENT

When a house gets to be about 20 years old (which is not old for a house) most things that need to be redone are kitchens and bathrooms. They are either too small for the modern lifestyle or the fixtures and appliances are outdated.

It isn't cheap to completely remodel a kitchen or a bath, especially if you plan to just gut it and replace everything. I say remodel wisely. It's a necessary evil to remodel both your kitchen a bath if you want to sell your home because the "other people" are doing it and if you want a chance to compete, you simply must do the same.

Baths, for instance, costs about half as much as a

kitchen for a complete remodeling job, maybe as much as $5,000. A kitchen might cost $10,000. These are the only two places where you have even a **chance** to get your money back from your remodeling investment.

Yet another item that seems to be "hot" at the moment is in having an office in your home. Some sellers took a room that was not being used (the living room that was replaced by the den or family room) and converted it into an office. I can't tell you how to arrange it so it doesn't stick out like a sore thumb; you make that decision.

Some owners built an office in their garage. They put up walls, paneled the outside, sheetrocked the inside, cut a hole in the side wall to install a heat pump (air and heat) and dropped in a smaller room with wash basin and toilet.

It was out of the house and away from noises. It was a definite positive to add to a home whether you use it or build it to appeal to others. It doesn't do anything to the square footage but, **it's another room!** It increased the **value** of the property.

Building an **apartment** on top of your garage will increase the value of your home. It adds square footage and can serve as maids quarters, a "private apartment-of sorts" for your teenager, or a place to put visiting in-laws. You know, it's comfortable enough but not so comfortable with those stairs to climb so they won't stay too long.

If you have room to add a second bath to an older 3-bedroom home that has but one bath, I'd say you have a chance to get your money back on that if the other homes in the neighborhood have only one bath.

But, a fireplace, new lawn and garden, deck, exterior paint, new heating or air conditioning system, extra insulation, skylight, or even paneling in or sheetrocking your garage won't increase your home **one red cent!**

It will, of course, make your property **sell faster** than the competition in your area, but it will not help your pocket-book. I've seen people throw their money away for years by thinking these improvements would increase the value of their home. They most emphatically **won't!**

STORY

I recently spent a considerable amount for a **swimming pool** for my backyard. I did it because I enjoy swimming and my kids love to swim. I feel, if I'm lucky, that I might recoup 10% of my investment when I sell my house because of this pool.

Then again, I might lose a sale because of it. My pool is heated and it's expensive to warm all that water. Too, many people don't want a pool because of the expense of maintaining it, or they're afraid of their kids drowning. I bought this pool for me and my family, not as a item to increase the value of my home.

STORY

A friend of mine built a **greenhouse** in his backyard, but again, only because he wanted it. One of these books I read talked about a greenhouse and stated that, *A greenhouse will add maybe 10% of it's construction cost to the value of your home.*

There's two ways to look at this also. It might raise the value to equal 10% of it's cost. Then, maybe not. If you live in a warm or hot climate, it will cost *mucho dinero* to **air condition,** and this greenhouse might just become a storage shed that is un-air conditioned!

If you put in things that you want, this doesn't necessarily mean **other** people want the same thing. Other than what I mentioned above, any expenses you make, you can just **kiss your investment goodby!**

I don't mean to be "cute" with this phraseology but it just happens to be raw truth. There are people who will sell you a new roof, vinyl siding or storm windows or storm doors and tell you, "This will increase the value of your home." I say *Horse Puckey.* It might make your home sell **faster** but it will not **increase** the value of it!

I'll cite an example, let's say you take two of the **exact homes** and put them side-by-side. One has this new metal roofing that costs $6000 more than the conventional roof. Which do you think will sell faster if the metal roof added $6000 to the selling price?

You know the answer to that one without hesitation. You'd buy the less expensive home with the "regular" roof. I know I would! A roof is not one of the top priorities or selling points in a house. If it looks good, if it doesn't leak, it's okay.

It's the same with **storm windows.** These windows are functional and attractive. Put the same two houses side-by-side, one that is $6000 more that has storm windows, and the other, $6000 less without, there's no big decision.

In order not to offend my friends at Ideal Roofing and Snap Screen, there will be some buyers (they'll say the ones with class) who will buy the homes with the metal roof and designer windows but the majority, uh-uh!

I feel that I talk for the majority of the people. I guess I'm one with no class because I'd choose the less expensive homes. Then later, you know, after you're in the (cheaper) home and you want to upgrade to this fancy roof or storm windows, that's fine but will they increase the value of your home? A most definite "no!"

SOME IMPROVEMENTS YOU HAVE TO MAKE

1.   A leaky or badly worn roof should be replaced or fixed. If not, you won't to get a good appraisal and probably not a mortgage loan.

2.   If your air conditioner (or heater) is not working, it must be repaired. You probably won't be able to get the money back that you put into these two items but

you'll never be able to sell the house if you don't.

3.   If your foundation has a problem; if it's cracked or the slab has sunk, it must be fixed and you'll not increase the value of your house one cent by doing this either. In fact, nothing that needs "fixing" will increase the value but, it must be done!

Keep your house clean, maintain it, if something breaks fix it but if you do something fancy to your home, do it because you want it and because it pleases you, but don't expect to get your money back out of it when it sells.

If the paint on the outside of your house is cracking, repaint it. But, no need to add new doors or windows or shutters because they won't increase the value of your home. If you want to add a skylight, know that it won't increase the value either; nor will extra insulation, a new thermostat, or finishing off an attic.

Whether you're buying a house or selling a house, you are having to move. I thought I'd give you a schedule to follow that will make life easier for both buyer and seller. The following chapter will give you some options, guidelines and reminders.

Part III

Chapter 11

YOU'VE BOTH GOT TO MOVE

I think everyone dreads moving; not necessarily the moving itself, this could be something you've all wanted, but the painstaking chore of packing then unpacking, leaving behind *junque* you never use but hate parting with, and the preparations that need to be made.

Weeks before, take a complete inventory of everything and decide what you will take and what you will leave, not only the large items but clothes and garden tools, including "stuff" that's been in your attic for the past ten years that you you have probably forgotten about.

In order to decide which furniture to take and which stays, it's a good idea to **draw a floor plan** of the home you are moving into. Try to make it fairly neat and reasonably accurate so you can make the right decisions.

Talk to your accountant, tax advisor or *H&R Block* agent on what you can give to *Good Will* or donate to the *Salvation Army.* On the items you don't want to give away, hold a garage sale and get what you can; anything is better than nothing. (When you reach your new destination, maybe turn the tables and shop at garage sales and pick up some of the same stuff you "gave away" or sold for ten cents on a dollar.)

Start packing the stuff you don't use every day at least **three weeks before** the moving date so you won't be rushed at the last minute. Look behind the front items in your refrigerator and pantry and discover things you had forgotten about and if edible, not green, or with visible "growing things" on it, eat it up.

Two weeks ahead of time, go to the post office and pick up a handful of *Change of Address cards* to notify friends, magazine companies, your bank, auto insurance company and anybody who mails things to you.

A **week or two** before you move make certain you take back any library books, have your vehicles checked and serviced and cancel your newspaper delivery. If you have prescriptions in a local pharmacy, get a copy of those for your new pharmacist, bring along any medical or dental records, and special items like car insurance papers, birth certificates or passports that might be in your bank vault.

If you're moving on your own, try to find boxes that are not to small or too large. You'll make what seems like a thousand trips with small boxes. And the larger ones will cause back strain or give you a hernia.

If you're using a professional mover, I know you have things that are precious to you. Box them yourself and watch over them, insured or not. Some items cannot be replaced or repaired and a check to repay a loss won't suffice.

The biggest decision you'll have to make other than moving and leaving some of your favorite furniture behind, is whether you are planning to move yourself or to use a professional mover. If you're going to make the long, dreaded trek to *wherever* on your own, this is my advice.

MOVING YOURSELF

If you have decided to move on your own, most families will need at least two large trucks (if you're taking it all) as well as your car and your spouses' van.

Once you make the decision who drives what, get estimates from a few truck rental companies and try to have an idea on how large a truck(s) you'll need.

When talking to these rental companies, ask them . . .

1.   Do you charge by the mile, day, size of truck, or any combination thereof?

2.   Do you sell packing boxes? If so, get the size and price.

3.   Do you have trucks with **automatic lift gates** and if so, how much additional for these?

4.   Do you have blankets I can use? If you rent them, how much and give me an idea on the size of the blanket?

5.   Do you have a dolly that comes with the rental or how much more to rent one?

I think that's sufficient information for you to make a decision to rent a truck or buy one and sell it when you get to wherever you're going. Call a few places to find out which suits you best.

A week or two before you are scheduled to pick up your truck, go to the rental agency and get one of their **contracts** to take home with you and read. **Read over the contract carefully!** It's like buying a house; if there's something you don't understand, ask!

In moving yourself, make certain you have the necessary *tools* to begin moving and packing such as:

1.   Reasonably sized boxes
2.   What is erroneously called Duct Tape, that large roll of silver tape that costs about $3.00 a roll.
3.   Sharp knife or large scissors.
4.   Blankets or furniture pads, large beach towels.
5.   Magic marker or self-stick labels.
6.   Lots of newspapers to crumple; avoids breakage.
7.   Hand truck or dolly.

USING A PROFESSIONAL MOVER

If you choose a professional mover, call at least three of the companies listed in the Yellow Pages for their rates and ask questions like . . .

1.   Do they supply packing boxes with the price they quoted?

2.   Do they have adequate insurance (I'm sure they do)? Then, what is the procedure for collecting claims and all details on that?

3.   What they expect you to pack and what will their movers pack?

4.   Is there an added charge on the packing?

5.   What method they accept for payment? Credit card, check, cashiers check, cash?

6.   At the destination, will the movers attempt to place your furniture where it goes?

7.   Is there a charge for **un**packing?

Have a large legal pad to list **every item** that is loaded into the truck. There will probably be someone else doing the same thing with the moving company. See if your records match before they drive off.

When the movers show up, as many of you as are in the family . . . be there! If you're taking your refrigerator have them load it first. Have it defrosted and cleaned before they arrive.

Walk along with the movers as they carry your

favorite piece of furniture to their truck. These movers are professionals but again, human beings, and some humans are less careful than others. All will be careful with a family member looking over their shoulder. Try not to nit-pick at them or they'll drop something on purpose and let the insurance cover it. Just make them aware that you're there.

Each company will have a Bill of Lading, marking off each item. As the items are moved from the truck into your new residence, be there with that list and check off each box and each piece of furniture.

Have it set so the last items they load are the first you'll need when you arrive at your destination. Items such as toilet paper, bath towels, tooth brushes (or is it teeth brushes assuming you have more than one tooth), coffee pot and cups, sugar or sweet & low, bed linen and a few pillows, and soap should be in your personal vehicle.

Everything else can wait to be unpacked but you want to be able to bathe, brush your teeth, use the toilet, and sleep. In the morning, you'll want that coffee before beginning to unpack.

When you arrive at your new home, call a locksmith and change the locks or add a dead bolt or two or those longer locks that are not easily pried open with a large screwdriver.

I know I must have forgotten something. My move from Florida over 8 years ago was an experience I will never forget. I'm listing the things I did and some I didn't. I also contacted a professional moving company a few days ago to update me.

LAGNIAPPE

This word, *lagniappe*, is a Louisiana *cajun* term meaning "something extra". Since we're nearing the end of this book, here is some "extra" information concerning moving.

EXPECT DELAYS

It's *Murphy's Law* again and things often go wrong that delay a closing. There are so many things that can go wrong at a closing that I would not plan on a moving date that was **carved in stone.**

It's a chain reaction. If an inspector finds a problem with the roof or slab, it must be repaired before you close. If there's a problem with the mortgage loan, there is a delay that affects both buyer and seller. If, at the last minute, either buyer or seller object to something—anything—the deal is postponed.

I think the saying, *"Don't count your chickens before they hatch"* was initiated by a farmer. With a Realtor, their saying is, *Don't count your money until the check clears the bank!*

Often, a home sale takes months to bring to fruition, and at the last minute, something goes wrong that negates the deal. Sometimes it can be remedied in minutes and sometimes it takes days or weeks.

Prepare yourselves for this, buyers and sellers. When you make your plans to move out and in, and something goes wrong to delay this move, don't be caught in the rain.

Chapter 12

EXEMPTIONS & TAXES AFTER AGE 65

Part of the following is taken from a form printed by the Harris County Appraisal District Information & Assistance Division in Houston, Texas. Their report is helpful and thorough and I don't think they'll mind my copying several of the key points.

I feel that all the information you can gather that will help you save money is a plus, and I will use every source and resource to help you do that. Each city and state has their own rules and you can call and get this information wherever you live.

The Appraisal District has 3 main responsibilities:

1. Identifying and placing a value on all taxable property, as of **January 1st** every year, according to market and productivity value.

2. To qualify the eligibility of exemptions applications for your homestead, those over 65 years of age, disability and disabled veterans.

3. Mentioning current ownership and appraisal records.

WHAT IS TAXABLE

To begin, the Appraisal District compiles a list of all

taxable property; homes, apartments, commercial buildings, shopping centers, vacant lots and land. Also, mobile homes, utilities and minerals such as oil and gas. In addition, vessels, certain vehicles and aircraft as well as business property used in the production of income. This includes furniture, fixtures, inventories and equipment.

HOW IT'S DONE

An appraiser periodically visits each property and records its size and other physical characteristics to set the value on it that is to be taxed. **Residential property** is normally appraised by comparing a given house to similar homes which have recently sold.

Property tax law requires that appraisals be *equal and uniform* and the same appraisal techniques must be used on similar properties. Property **cannot be appraised differently just because a property owner is over the age of 65!** This means the **appraisal is the same**, but you have special exemptions. Read on.

WHO TAXES YOU

Your appraisal district only establishes a fair market value on your property. **Elected officials** in the county, cities, schools, districts do the actual setting of the amount to collect these taxes.

Now that you know how it's done and by whom, let's see how those of you who are over six-and-a-half decades old can get some of these exemptions.

EXEMPTIONS FOR THE OVER-65

If you reach (or pass) age 65 by January 1st you are entitled to an **Over-65 homestead exemption!** All **school districts** will then grant you an additional reduction of $10,000 from the appraised value of your home.

Make certain you apply for this exemption when you are eligible. When the appraisal district is aware of your age status, (you write and tell them) this information goes to all the taxing units.

Once you receive your Over-65 homestead exemption, you automatically qualify for a **tax ceiling** on school taxes. Unless, you build an additional room, or enclose a patio or sun room, covert an attached garage into a living area, your **school taxes cannot increase** as long as you own the home and live in it.

If you make any improvements other than normal repairs or maintenance (replacing a roof is maintenance; installing piers to level a slab is repairs and these are accepted) but anything additional will mean your **school tax ceiling** will be recalculated.

Let's say your school tax ceiling is $550 on your present homestead, and you add a 15 x 20 foot game room that increases the square footage and the value on your house. This is an improvement other than normal repairs or maintenance and your school tax will rise ($52) to $602.

Your **tax ceiling** isn't now gone, only increased to a higher ceiling because of the added value of your home. This new ceiling will be in effect from this year onward.

When a homeowner who's been receiving the tax ceiling dies, the ceiling will transfer to the surviving spouse —**if**—that spouse is at least 55 years old. This is not an automatic transfer, the spouse must **apply to the appraisal district** and this ceiling applies for as long as the spouse lives in the home.

DISABLED HOMEOWNER WHO IS OVER 65

There's a "kicker" here. If you are disabled and you receive disability benefits, you can't have both homestead exemptions; you must **choose** one or the other, whichever is to your best interest.

DISABLED VETERAN WHO IS OVER 65

Disabled veterans, their surviving spouses, and surviving minor children may receive an exemption which may be applied to any **single piece of taxable property!** The exemptions range from $1,500 to $3,000 depending on the degree of **service connected disability** for which Veterans Administration benefits are received.

A disabled veteran **over the age of 65** qualifies for the full $3,000 if their disability rating is at least ten percent. This exemption would be **in addition** to other Over-65 homestead exemptions.

HOW TO FILE FOR THIS EXEMPTION

Look in your telephone directory for your Appraisal District office and they will mail you an application. Fill out only one application for all of the homestead exemptions you qualify for. After you've filled out this form, mail it back after January 1st but not later than April 30th.

> If you live in a mobile home, send in a copy of the title along with your application.

Disabled veterans get a separate application. Once you apply for a Disabled Veterans' exemption, you don't have to apply again unless the appraisal office asks you to do so in writing or unless your qualifications change. For instance, if you move into a new home, you must file a new application and advise the office to cancel the exemption of your former home.

OVER-65 HOMESTEAD TAX DEFERRAL

Homeowners aged 65 or over can defer, or postpone, paying current and delinquent property taxes on their homestead for as long as they own it and live in it! Again, call the office and have them send you and Over-65 Homestead Tax Deferral Affidavit.

If you've **already been sued** for delinquent taxes owed on your homestead, the lawsuit can be halted by filling the Deferral Affidavit with the court in which the suit is pending. This applies to all taxing units that tax your homestead.

This Deferral Affidavit means that as long as you live in the home, the property **cannot be sold for delinquent taxes** and you **can't be forced to move!** This, only **postpones** the payment of these taxes, it **does not cancel them!** Taxes, penalties and interest are **due** if you no longer own or live in that home and taxing units will file a lawsuit that the new homeowner of the estate must pay if they want to retain the property.

Note: A homeowner may file a Tax Deferral upon reaching age 65; it isn't necessary to wait until January 1st.

PAYING TAXES AFTER AGE 65

Recognizing that a growing number of people are over 65 years of age, the government has some tax relief in the form of new "payment options". You can pay for your taxes with your Visa or Mastercard.

Isn't that one big relief? This means if you **don't have the money** you can **charge it** and pay the added interest! Not only that, this big **"relief"** entitles the taxing unit to add a **processing fee** to the credit card payment. What bright governing body or legislator came up with that piece of garbage? Are we paying people to make these "concessions" to the elderly, most of whom are on a fixed income?

By contract with the property owner, tax collectors

may establish an **escrow account** for receiving monthly payments toward the owner's future taxes (same as an escrow account mortgage companies usually set out when you buy your home). This is sort of a forced savings plan, which I don't think is a bad idea.

You can make **installment payments** on these taxes. If you pay at least one-fourth of the tax bill before the February 1st delinquent date, you may pay the remainder, **without penalty,** in three equal installments prior to April 1st, June 1st and August 1st.

HOWEVER, if a payment is missed, the remainder of tax due becomes immediately delinquent and is subject to penalty and interest charges. Since I live in Harris County, I am going to give you their numbers:

Harris County Tax Officials . . . 224-1919
City of Houston Tax Officials . . 861-5700
Houston ISD Tax Officials 861-6024

TAXES WHEN YOU SELL YOUR HOME

Income tax is a determining factor in almost every business deal. When selling your home, there are two things that happen; either you realize a net loss on the sale and owe no tax, or you'll realize a profit and you'll owe tax.

Let's first talk about what you can **deduct** to lower this tax obligation. The answer is **every expense you can think of!** The government can only collect on the pure profit you made when selling your home.

In fact, you can deduct the extra costs you paid when moving in and you can also deduct the costs of moving out! Mark down on one page, first, the **original price** you paid for your home. That's a large amount.

Be certain to add any monies you might have paid at that time which includes attorney's fees, escrow fees, notary fees, title inspection fees, property inspection costs, surveys, and any and all closing costs you paid, even moving expenses way back when.

Next, add the cost of any capital improvements you might have made such as new roof, sprinkler system, air conditioner, room addition etc. Do not add small items over the past 15 years like replacing a window, a new faucet or painting; these expenses are normal to maintain the condition of your home.

When you sold the house, list these costs also, like real estate commission, attorney's fees, and closing costs you agreed to make, cost of surveys, inspections, and advertising costs. For the repairs you make in order to sell this house, you can subtract all the fix-up costs including painting, new windows, remodeling a bath or kitchen, etc. The work must be done during the **90 days before** you signed the contract and paid for no later than **30 days after** you closed the sale.

When all is said and done, you take the costs involved in the initial purchase, then the cost to sell your home, against the amount you received. Assuming you made a **profit,** you owe tax on this profit. If you show a **loss**, of course you don't owe any taxes but you also won't be able to take a deduction against other earned income from this loss. Hey! I'm sorry for this. I don't make the rules, I'm only telling you about them.

Let's talk about **avoiding** paying tax even if you do **make a profit** from the sale of your home. You can defer paying taxes on the profit you made by purchasing a home that costs the same amount of money you received (including profit) on the home you sold, or one that costs **more!** You have two years in which to do this.

If you purchase a new home for **less** than what you sold your previous home for, you owe tax on the difference. Here's a big plus for those of you who are over 55 years of age; you may be eligible for a one-time exclusion that allows you to keep up to $125,000 of your resale profits, tax-free! The only stipulation is that you must have used the home as your primary residence for at least three of the past five years.

Of course, tax laws are complex and likely to change. Ask your Realtor if they are up on this. Most are. If not, consult your CPA or tax attorney.

People are living longer these days. The population of senior citizens today is greater than ever before in recorded history. Many live on fixed incomes and are unable to meet their financial obligations including mounting property tax burdens.

Property taxes are **local** taxes governed by State law that fund **public services**. They pay for fire and police protection, medical and hospital care for the poor and indigent, public education, flood control projects, parks and recreational facilities, road and street maintenance, clean drinking water, and sewage disposal as well as many other expenses that make our life more comfortable.

These laws are the laws of men (and women) and that is why I implore you—those of you over as well as under the age of 65—to look into these laws. Know what you are being charged for and why. Knowledge is your foremost weapon.

The other is your vote! Vote for the legislators whom you feel will give you the best "run for your money" then cross your fingers, maybe say a prayer and hope for the best.

I truly do love and appreciate this country. It is, without exception, the greatest country in the world. I also happen to believe that the majority of government, state and local officials are, basically, good people. I think they are doing and have tried to do whatever it is that is to the best interest of all the citizens of the United States in accordance with The Constitution.

However, I don't like giving anyone *Carte Blanche* over all aspects of my life, and the only way to guard against this is by learning. Then, we have a chance to change things that we deem unfair. Look back. I said "chance" to change things. It doesn't mean we can, but without this knowledge, we never have this chance?

* * * * *

In my books and over radio and television, I fight for what I believe is right. If a product (in my estimation as a so-called expert) is inferior, or a guarantee is bogus, I'll tell you about it. And if a manufacturer of a product or service personnel tell you something that is questionable in your mind, get a second opinion if my book(s) don't cover it.

Each and every one of you reading this book can count on a few things from me. First, I'll tell you the truth! I am unafraid of any consequences because I will not prostitute myself or my beliefs for any reason and I will never compromise my integrity.

Second, if I don't know about something you ask, I'll tell you so. I keep current on most things concerning building, remodeling, maintenance and home repair but I don't know it all!

Third, I will not endorse a product or company that I have not either had or heard many positive reports on. Every day I get calls from companies, businesses and individuals who ask me to endorse their product. If (again in my estimation) it's good, I'll do it. And if not, I'll say why and try not to feel badly about it.

Oftentimes, I've had individuals reproach me, asking why I say things or "knock" a product. Because, that's what I do! That's my job. I make a living helping people repair, maintain, build, buy or sell a home. I don't want to hurt any business, product or individual. But, I refuse to endorse or recommend a product that is faulty.

I will always give them examples of why their product is not good for this area or region in a clear, concise, academic, proven manner. Many of these folks are nice, honest individuals but they have no gripe with me; their gripe is with the manufacturer of the product they are selling!

Homeowners, home-buyers, home-sellers, builders, remodelers, those of you who want to maintain your homes or make repairs, I am for you! I work daily to get this information to you so that you can make an informed decision. Oops! Time to get of my soapbox. Just know that I care.

Good luck, thank you for buying my book(s) and may God bless you.

Tom Tynan

ADDITIONAL INFO FOR BUYER **AND** SELLER

I've listed a bunch of things I suggest the **seller** do prior to putting his/her home up for sale, many with cleaning and making minor repairs.

This also pertains to the buyer because as new homeowners, there will always be things that need replacing, refurbishing or repairing, most of which, you can do yourself and save money.

The easy answer is to buy my first book, **HOME IMPROVEMENT.** It answers hundreds of questions all homeowner's need to know. This book did so well, and continues to do well, that in less than 18 months it is into it's fifth printing. Yeah, I like that.

There are thousands of "little" things that can go wrong in your home that you can repair easily, and in my **HOME IMPROVEMENT** book, I covered as many of the minor everyday problems space would allow.

I plan to have my **fourth** book out **(STEP BY STEP)** before the end of 1995 that will take you though many of the bigger problems that you can (mostly) handle yourself. It too, will save you headache, heartache, time, and a **lot** of money!

Again, thanks for buying my book. I hope you have all of them. If not, they are in most bookstores throughout the country or you can order them by writing or calling the publisher. The information is on the last page of this book.

OTHER BOOKS BY SWAN PUBLISHING

HOW NOT TO BE LONELY . . . If you're about to marry, recently divorced or widowed, want to forgive, forget or both, this is an excellent book to read. Candid, positive, entertaining and informative. If you're looking for a new person, this tells **where** to find them, **what** to say and **how to keep them** once you get them. (over 2 million copies sold) . . . . $ 9.95

HOW NOT TO BE LONELY <u>TONIGHT</u> . . . aimed at the *MALE* reader. Other than being courageous and strong, smart women want their man to be sensitive, caring, and understanding. "The" book to give to your man. Or, for men who really want to learn what turns the modern woman on. A fun book for your coffee table . . . . . $ 9.95

NEW FATHER'S BABY GUIDE . . . The "perfect" gift for ALL new fathers. Tells (dummy dad) about lamaze classes, burping, feeding and changing the baby plus 40 side-splitting drawings. Most of all, it tells dad how to **SPOIL** mom! Mothers, sisters, girl friends, grandmothers, **get this book for dad, he needs it!** . . . . . . $ 9.95

YOUR FRONT YARD . . . A fun book of information by garden expert John Burrow. It tells about plants, trees, grass, pesticides, fertilizer, lawn and garden maintenance, **everything** you need to know to plant or keep a beautiful front yard . . . . $ 9.95

VEGETABLE GARDENING (Spring and Fall) . . . is yet another fine, fun book written by John Burrow. It tells the size garden you need to feed your family, which vegetables grow best for a country, city, and even an apartment garden on your patio or in planters, and for you "cool" folks, herb gardens to impress your friends . . . $9.95

REVERSING IMPOTENCE FOREVER . . . by Dr. David Mobley and Dr. Steven Wilson, world renowned urologists who specialize in impotence. This book tells it **all**, and includes diagrams as well as numbers to call for additional information and/or help. It *can* change your sex life for the better. **Women** buy this book 50 to 1 over men. Men, find out what you need to know . . . . $ 9.95

KEEP IT UP . . . A book co-authored by Dr. Mobley and writer/producer and fitness guru John Pepe on how to **prevent** impotence. It's not a crime to suffer from this problem but it is extremely unwise to not do anything to prevent it. Men, if you're under 40, get this book. If you're **over** 40, get this one and the one above. There are some amazing things to learn that most men aren't aware of . . . . $ 9.95

QUEST FOR MEGALODON . . . An adventure book written by ocean engineer Tom Dade about a supposedly extinct shark that ruled the oceans more than 50 million years ago. A physician, a Hall of Fame baseball player and an oceanographer, once boyhood fishing buddies, reunite for the adventure of a lifetime. *JAWS* was 20 feet long and weighed 3 tons. Megaladon is **100** feet long and weighs upwards of **60** tons! (About to be made into a movie) $12.95

HOW TO BUY A NEW CAR AND SAVE THOUAND *And how to sell or trade your old one* . . . Cliff Evans, twenty year veteran in sales and management in the retail car business, shares the "innermost secrets" of what car dealerships **don't** want you to know. This information will educate the consumer of sales techniques, financing facts and can save the new car buyer time *and* money . . . . $ 9.95

* If you can't find these books in retail outlets, write or call us to order by check or credit card. Our address and telephone numbers are on the following page. On books listed above, add $2.90 **per book** for shipping and handling. Expect delivery within 7-10 days.

TOM TYNAN is available for personal appearances, luncheons, banquets, home shows, seminars, etc. He is entertaining and informative. Call **(713) 388-2547** for cost and availability.

For a copy of *Vol 1, HOME IMPROVEMENT with Tom Tynan, Vol 2, BUILDING & REMODELING with Tom Tynan or Vol 3, BUYING A HOME & SELLING A HOME by Tom Tynan,* send a personal check or money order in the amount of $12.85 per copy to:
Swan Publishing
126 Live Oak,
Alvin, TX, 77511
Please allow 7-10 days for delivery.

To order by major credit card 24 hours a day call:
(713) 268-6776 or long distance **1-800-TOM-TYNAN.**

Libraries—Bookstores—Quantity Orders:

Swan Publishing
126 Live Oak
Alvin, TX 77511

Call **(713) 388-2547**
FAX **(713) 585-3738**